Contemporary Theology Series

Marxism
&
Christianity

HANS-LUTZ POETSCH

MARXISM AND CHRISTIANITY

CONTEMPORARY THEOLOGY SERIES

MARXISM AND CHRISTIANITY

Hans-Lutz Poetsch

Edited by Paul Schmiege

Publishing House
St. Louis London

Concordia Publishing House, St. Louis, Missouri
Concordia Publishing House Ltd., London E. C. 1
Copyright © 1973 Concordia Publishing House
Library of Congress Catalog Card No. 78-82690
ISBN 0-570-06724-3

MANUFACTURED IN THE UNITED STATES OF AMERICA

CONTENTS

PREFACE

Marx's Communist theories are more than a century old. Only minori-
ies reacted favorably to them during his lifetime. The founder of that
special ideology suffered the experience that his theories did not lead
the several revolutions in Western Europe of his time to successful
conclusions. The philosopher and fighter finally died as a poor man
in his London exile. The First International broke asunder; the Second
International Workers Association was killed by World War I, when
its members — contrary to their common socialist convictions — decided
to fight against each other as soldiers in the armies of their respective
nations.

Today Marxistic Communism rules more than half of mankind.
It is also invading nations of the western hemisphere: hardly a country
is without an active Communist party. The ideology is gaining more
and more positive interest and fascination, especially among intellectuals. The brutality of the political program and practice within its
own realms does not dim its attraction for the poor and even for the
wealthy in other lands.

Marxism is divided into several schools, and some of them fight
against each other with philosophical and political means. Red China,
Soviet Russia, and Yugoslavia are examples of such conflicts. It is evident that ideological sectarianism evolves whenever the strict rule of
law dominates principles of thinking and action. The human understanding of law and order is changing with the changing times, and
that change influences the interpretation of a respective philosophy
or belief.

Marxism is not only an economic and/or socialist philosophy, but
also a belief. One may call it a pseudo-religion. The conviction among
the founders of Communism of having a real mission to mankind
should not be overlooked. Marxism retains this character even today.
When we attempt to argue with real Communists we find that we are
disputing with fanatic representatives of an atheistic and materialistic
religion hidden behind an assertion of real scientific foundation. This
statement does not militate against discussions with Communists; it
does show, however, that no persuasion is possible through rational
(philosophical) arguments alone. If discussion with Communists is
to make any sense at all, it can only take place with the aim of con-
verting the protagonist.

The effectiveness of Marxism must be understood against the back-
ground of failures of Christendom in many nations. The system came
into existence in the midst of secularized Christian nations, and it is

7

still a reaction against some depravities in that society, for instance, the exploitation of certain classes. But it is not only a reaction. Marx, with some other philosophers of his time, believed that he could discover the real root of Christianity in the self-deception of oppressed peoples. However, he offered a concept for the benefit of mankind, which, according to him, was based upon irrefutable scientific truth and therefore had to be implemented. Marx taught the evolution of mankind before Charles Darwin brought forth his well-known theories; and the later Communists adopted Darwin's evolutionism as a central part of their ideology.

It is often said that Marxism is a special kind of secularized Christianity. This may be correct to a certain extent. But our conclusions will be false if we think of that ideology as being something that "apes Christianity." This is out of the question. Every development based upon God's gift of the Gospel will follow an entirely different route from a system which is dependent on an immanent understanding of law only. It is correct to say that Christianity involves some "social" aspects (for example, in its perception of a congregation), and that Marxism owns an atheistic eschatology. The parallels in the two, however, dare not mislead our judgment. We correctly conclude that Marxism is essentially bound to religion, especially Christianity, as its negation. The Christian understanding of life is the necessary antithesis of Marxism, while most other world religions are prone to accommodate to that ideology.

We can hardly give a full picture of the phenomenon of Marxism on the following few pages. It is rather our aim to offer an introduction to the classic thoughts of Karl Marx with special consideration of the Communists' most famous document, the *Communist Manifesto*. We will treat the arguments which have to be repudiated from the Christian point of view. Last but not least, we dare not close our minds to Marxism's correct evaluation of the failures of Christianity.

Chapter 1

The Personality of Karl Marx

THE ROOTS OF MARXISM

Different factors can be named which influenced Marx's way of thinking: his personal origin, his opposition or adaptation of Friedrich Hegel's philosophical system, and his personal experiences as a reporter and editor of the *Rhinelandic Newspaper*.

1. Marx's Origin

Karl Marx was born May 5, 1818, in Trier. His father was a Jewish advocate, Hirschel Marx, while his mother (Henrietta *nee* Presberg) was descended from an old Dutch family of rabbis. The parents were open to the philosophers and poets of the Enlightenment.

The French Revolution of 1789 has to be considered as the most important political success of the Enlightenment. Here the Jews gained their emancipation in society. At that time Trier belonged to France. After Napoleon I was defeated, the Congress of Vienna (1815) gave the town to Prussia, and the Jews lost their rights again. Hirschel Marx, therefore, converted to Protestantism and accepted the name Heinrich. This conversion allowed him to enter positions in government service and to move in the cultural circles of the European world.

Already in his childhood Karl Marx found that philosophical liberalism was able to attain freedom for those religious groups which were considered to be second class in society. By contrast, a conservative society stamped by Christian tradition was not ready to intercede for oppressed minorities but often turned back the wheel of history (as happened, for example, in Prussia). The Jewish emancipation had to be reached by revolution, which for Marx seemed to be the only means of changing social structures. He himself had had his first contact with the Prussian state police when he was still a high school student and one of his teachers proclaimed ideals of freedom which disturbed Prussian conservativism.

Christian students of Marxism, like Helmut Gollwitzer, have raised the question whether atheism is an unconditional element in that ideology. We will have to answer this question later, but we want to direct attention to Marx's very early experiences, which cannot be excluded from his system. He did not want to be a philosopher only but also a fighter for improvement of society by radical change. Therefore his thoughts cannot be judged only in a rational way. He struggled

11

for the liberation of the enslaved proletariat, which suffered its miseries without opposing them. Philosophy may demonstrate the absurdity of the human conditions of its time and then help to develop the more ideal social structures of the future, which must inevitably come.

2. Marx's Philosophical Development

After years of study at Bonn University, Karl Marx moved to Berlin in 1836. He mastered numerous disciplines such as law, philosophy, literature, history of arts, mathematics, Latin, English, and Italian. Hegel's philosophy was taught in a strongly conservative manner, and although Marx refuted Hegel, he nevertheless came under the influence of Hegel's way of thinking.

Marx's relation to Friedrich Hegel (d. 1831), in combination with Ludwig Andreas Feuerbach (1804–1872) is of primary importance to the research on Marxism in the western hemisphere. Hegel's idealist system can be considered an exclusive highlight in modern philosophy. Indeed, the question may be asked as to how far even existentialism and other philosophical schools of our time are in principle really contingent on this great thinker. Hegel's intellectual system asserts that everything which is reality has to be understood as "rational." Philosophy and religion have the same common object; this appears in religion as the lower form of conception (Vorstellung), while philosophy acts with it in the higher form of idea (idee). Thus theology and philosophy were seemingly reconciled to each other, and Hegel's system consequently won wide influence in Christianity. Men like Feuerbach (and Marx) might in reverse have looked at Christianity through the glasses of Hegel's understanding. Modern philosophical research, for instance, asks whether Feuerbach's atheism is directed against God or against Hegel's definition of "God" as absolute spirit or absolute idea. Whatever the case might be, we say that in our time most of the thinkers who tried to develop Hegel's system fell into an anti-Christian atheism. (Søren Kierkegaard might be mentioned as the most important exception to this classification.)

Feuerbach defined Hegel's system as a masked theology, which is transformed into logic. Philosophy, however, dare not start with the act of thinking but must begin with the whole of living. The vivid truth of the sensual thus replaces exclusive thinking. Marx credited Feuerbach as being the man who overcame Hegel's philosophy and gave three reasons: (1) He proved that philosophy is nothing other than theology transformed into thought; (2) he made the social relations of human beings with one another, and thereby true materialism of real knowledge, the basic principle of the theory; (3) he established the positive as that which is sensually certain and positively based in itself. This was in opposition to Hegel's negation, which falsely pretends to be the absolute positive; for Hegel starts with the infinite, the abstract general, namely with religion and theology, then abrogates the infinite and sets in its stead the sensual, the real, the finite, and the special. Later on he suspends the positive again and rehabilitates the abstract and the infinite. Feuerbach opposed this whole line of thought with his sensually certain position, which is based upon itself (cf. Marx's "National Economy and Philosophy," in *Die Fruehschriften,* Kroener, p. 250 ff.).

We have already anticipated history in mentioning Marx's judgment of Feuerbach's attack against Hegel, for the cited contribution was published in 1844. However, we see that several philosophers among the systematicians of the 19th century tried to disengage themselves from this Berlin giant. Karl Marx was connected with the doctors' club, the "Young Hegelians," and for several years was a close friend of radical theologian Bruno Bauer. In 1841 he received the doctor of philosophy degree at Jena University with his dissertation on the difference between Democritus' and Epicurus' philosophy of nature. He then began to develop his criticism of Hegel's system using the terms of Feuerbach's critical contribution. Whether Marx was really influenced by this famous atheistic thinker is still under discussion. A statement of Friedrich Engel's is often cited, according to which the liberating effect of Feuerbach's *Essence of Christianity* gave enthusiasm to everybody in his group. But it is asserted with sound reasons that this is also true of Marx. He appreciated many of the individual arguments but did not follow Feuerbach so far in his individualism.

Feuerbach, until he accepted the I-You relation, saw man as an abstract being. He seemed to feel that society might be endangered by an upcoming nihilism and therefore changed his material relation of love (*Liebesbeziehung*) into an order of love. This order has to be understood in a worldly religious manner. (Remember the opposite road; Hegel went along with changing the term "love," which he used at the beginning, into "spirit.") Marx did not speak of the individual but gave man a sociological interpretation: "The being of man is not determined by his consciousness, but his consciousness by his social being." ("Preface to the Political Economy.")

Feuerbach's late religiosity owes a certain relationship to Comte: the so-called "positivistic consequence" brought up the paradox of "religious atheism" (E. Thier). Marx did not go this way but remained an atheist. His ideas were aimed at a distant target—not founded on a criticism of Hegel.

3. Marx's First Journalistic Experiences

The *Rhinelandic Newspaper* was a Prussian periodical in opposition to the Roman Catholic and anti-Prussian *Cologne Newspaper.*

It was transformed quite soon into a voice of middle-class democracy in the sense of the French Revolution with its stand against the Prussian "enlightened despotism." The first issue of this *Rhinelandic Newspaper* appeared on January 1, 1842; Marx became its editor-in-chief in October. The organ was forbidden by the Prussian government at the end of 1843.

Marx's involvement in that journalistic work was of importance to his further development for three reasons:

1. He opposed the Prussian censorship and voted for freedom of the press; a press which, he argued, could not be considered as a trade.

2. He became acquainted with the real economic situation of the lower-class people through lawsuits for thefts of wood. The poor farmhands and their families lived according to the customary law, which allowed the collection of wood in the forests; this was forbidden by the farmers and landlords when wood became more expensive on the market. Only the landed classes could speak in the parliament of the county—but not the poor people who were concerned. The journalist Karl Marx in his periodical was the only one who defended the interests of the poor population. In this case Marx probably met economic reality for the first time as an essential factor of human existence of his time.

3. The first socialist movements became better known in these years. We think especially of the (Christian) socialists at Paris like Wilhelm Weitling (*The Gospel of the Poor Sinners*, 1843), Félicité Robert de la Mennais (*Words of a Believer*), Pierre Joseph Proudhon (*What Does Property Mean?* 1840), and the English socialist reformer Robert Owen (founder of the first general labor union in 1834). Last but not least, we must mention the Russian revolutionary and anarchist Michail Alexandrovitch Bakunin, who stood for the abolition of state, religion, and marriage.

Marx's First Stay in Paris

From the end of October 1843 Marx lived in Paris. He came with his friend Arnold Ruge in order to win the radically oriented Frenchmen to cooperation in the planned publication of a bilingual periodical. Only one double-issue was edited: *French-German Yearbooks*, with two contributions by Marx: "Concerning the Problem of the Jews" and "Concerning Criticism on Hegel's Philosophy of Law."

> The state is, according to Hegel, the creator of the reasonable and moral orders on the political and social level; society, therefore, results from the state.

> On the contrary, Marx taught that social powers determine the state; criticism of the state has to be transformed into a criticism of society. Proletariat and philosophy shape a union: "As philosophy

14

finds its material weapons in the proletariat, so the proletariat finds its mental and spiritual weapons in philosophy."

Marx's impression of the French socialist groups was very negative. He observed that they were confused and diverging from each other. But he met with one man who became his closest friend and the co-founder of Marxism: FRIEDRICH ENGELS.

Engels was born in 1820 at Barmen, the oldest of eight children of a strongly pietistic factory owner. While studying at Bremen, he became influenced by the left wing of Hegel's followers. Although he began to attack Pietism, he did not leave his Christian group until he read David Friedrich Strauss' book *Life of Jesus,* which can be judged as the first extremely rationalistic publication. The basic dogmas of Christianity are denied in it, and the fundamental reports of the Gospels are explained as myths. Through the influence of this publication Engels' belief received its decisive push, and he became a convinced Communist. His change of mind was also influenced by experiences Engels gathered during his stay in one of his father's factories in Manchester, England. He recognized that the left wing of Hegel's followers was correct in its statement that the miseries of the poor people are the preconditions of the wealth of the rich classes. Economic facts play an important role in the modern world. They give the basis for the origin of social class contrasts in industrial countries. Economic facts are the basis of the foundation of political parties and of their fights—and therefore for the whole political history. Engels intensively studied the system of economy. At this time labor problems were discussed in public as shown by Robert Owen's works and the fight for the rights of labor unions, by the riot of the Silesian weavers, etc.

Engels' contribution "Outlines to a Criticism of National Economy" (1844) had quite an influence on Marx's further thought. The former Pietist experienced the extreme English capitalism with its wealth and superfluity on one side and depravity and misery on the other. Those paradoxes seemed to be caused by commercial competition. Therefore it was necessary that mercantilism with its monopolies be completely overthrown in order to demonstrate the real consequences of private property: the separation of capital and labor from capital and gain, and from interest and gain. The acceptance of interest without labor was immoral. Labor was seen as separate from capital, and wages separated it anew from its product. Only the abolition of private property could help to again give labor its due wage. However, the economic structure of the capitalistic era was evolving. According to Engels, in the final state of the process there would only be some millionaires, wealthy landlords, and a crowd of poor laborers.

It is evident that Engels started his work on the basis of practical experience, while Marx began with a philosophical criticism of Hegel's idealist system. Marx received a mighty impulse when both men met in Paris, and from now on he studied standard national economics works diligently.

We should mention another socialistic thinker, who influenced Marx to a certain extent: the "Communist rabbi" MOSES HESS.

> He was born in Bonn in 1812, grew up in the Jewish tradition, and studied at Bonn University after having quarreled with his father. He lived in the Netherlands, Belgium, France, and Switzerland and was always in contact with the beginning laborers' movement and with socialist writers. He often seemed to be entirely influenced by contemporary philosophies, but he thereby clothed his own feelings and thoughts. He became acquainted with Marx (and Engels) in 1841 and was, like those two, convinced that socialism would come. He longed for action, and in this respect stood close to Bakunin and Lassalle. Later on he was a member of the I International. He finally turned back to the Jewish Zionist movement, to which he then devoted his whole energy.

Hess wrote that the religion of love and humanity found in every human being has to be confessed (cf. his "Communist Confession" of 1844 or 1845). It is the fulfillment of the Christian religion, the meaning and aim of which is the happiness of the whole of mankind through love, freedom, and righteousness. Christianity did not achieve its aim, because it imagined the content of its faith figuratively, that is, the suffering of mankind in the picture of the crucified Son of Man. Perfection is not reached before the heavenly joys come. The Communist society, however, brings heaven on earth: it lives in loving instead of hating and being egotistically oriented. Man is good, but the world is bad and infects man; money is considered the incarnation of evil; and hell is the description of life under the mastery of money. God, who is nothing other than love, is the real life. Thus God is mankind united in love. What is called "religion" here can also be termed "atheism" as long as its substance is preserved, namely a real chiliastic breakthrough into this world.

Marx became influenced by Hess's contributions in Herwegh's *21 Pages From Switzerland* (1843), in which that which Hess in former and later years defined as religion is called atheism. A nation is not free in its mentality as long as it is materially enslaved; a god in the beyond is, therefore, permanently an expression of this state. Religion numbs the active energy, which reacts against disasters and tries to liberate from evil. Religion is only able to serve like opium in painful maladies. There is no more than a formal difference between intellectual and social slavery or between the religious and political way of government; the first attempts to reduce man to a transcendental-earthly power, the other—to an earthly-transcendental might. Both destroy every godly energy and freedom in man and in the world—in spirit and in objective creations alike. Real freedom can only be gained after religion and the state are overcome. Thus Communism surpasses the former revolutionary philosophy, which negated the state only as a contemporary phenomenon but not in its basic sense.

Hegel recognized that man's freedom is not to be sought in the individualistic factor but in that which is common to all men. Property cannot promote personal freedom, if it is not a common possession. One's own inviolable property can only be considered as such, if it is a common good. Proudhon presented the correct definition when he answered the question of the character of property with the words: "Property is larceny." Marx's work *National Economy and Philosophy* demonstrates Hess's influence upon his thoughts. Erich Thier states: "Since Marx met with Moses Hess, the period of existential Hegel-criticism has been overcome; possibility has become necessity" (*Das Menschenbild des jungen Marx*, p. 61). Hess worked together with Marx and Engels at the "German Ideology" while they lived in Brussels (1845-46); he later parted company with them and went his own way.

FURTHER IMPORTANT DATES IN MARX'S LIFE

Prussia was able to convince the French government to banish the four most hated co-workers on the Communist periodical written for Switzerland and Germany: *Vorwaerts*. Marx had to leave France and went to Brussels, Belgium, in the beginning of 1845. But he came back to Paris in 1848, after a successful revolution of liberal republicans against "citizen king" Louis Philippe and his conservative statesman Guizot; at that time the Belgian government considered expelling Marx from its country. The new French government established by republicans and socialists asked him to devise a program with clear demands and to unite men able to realize it. The famous *Communist Manifesto* with its ten paragraphs was the result of Marx's work. With Willem Banning we can summarize its content as follows:

1) The economic production and—as the necessary consequence— the social partition of every historical period forms the basis for the political and intellectual history of this period.

2) The whole of history is a history of class conflict between the exploited and the gainers—between the ruled classes and the ruling classes—on the different levels of social development.

3) This war has reached the point at which the proletariat is no longer able to free itself from the bourgeoisie without delivering the whole society forever from exploitation, oppression, and class conflict.

The same year that the revolutionary movements reached Berlin and Vienna, Marx turned back to the Rhineland. He founded the *New Rhinelandic Newspaper* and took over the leadership of the party cell of Communists in Cologne, a cell which had been as badly organized there as everywhere else. Marx's conception was the following one: The predominance of feudalism and conservativism must first be broken in order to bring the bourgeoisie, urged on and supported by the proletariat, to rule. Both classes have to establish one front as long as the bourgeoisie remains revolutionary. This front will fall asunder when conservativism is destroyed; then the proletariat will also turn against the progressive bourgeoisie in order to reach its final revolutionary aim, namely, the expropriation of private property.

When the revolutionary flood slackened, the *New Rhinelandic Newspaper* lost the financial support of its investors and was finally forbidden by the government. (The last issue was published on May 19, 1849.) Marx was brought to court and accused of agitation. He defended himself by delivering a kind of lecture on the historic-materialistic task of the revolutionary movement: 1848 demonstrated the fight of the old feudal-bureaucratic powers against the modern bourgeois society; a war of free competition against the corporations, the landed property, and the industry; and the struggle of science against belief. A social revolution was taking place behind those events. The judges absolved Marx from the accusation of agitation, but he was expelled by the government. He moved to London because Brussels and Paris would not accept him. He lost his and his wife's total possessions in order to pay the debts of the *New Rhinelandic Newspaper*. From now on he was totally without means.

The general situation refuted Marx's theory. Power remained steadfastly in the hands of his enemies. Marx and Engels tried again to create a means for their ideas in Germany. In February 1850 the *New Rhinelandic Newspaper, Political-Economic Revue*, was published at Hamburg. But their hopes were in vain; the last issue came out in November with Marx's statement of accounts. According to it the economic crisis of the preceding years was being overcome in favor of activity and wealth. One could not speak of a real revolution under those circumstances, because revolution was only possible in connection with a new crisis. In time that would come and with it the revolution. Thus Marxism was built on a strategy determined by scientific insight into the lawfulness of economic evolution.

Karl Marx began again with an intensive study of English economic literature in the British Museum. He studied the research of the parliament into the labor situation and observed international politics and history. The conditions of his life were unbearable; he earned nothing, and three children died. In 1859 the first part of his famous book *Capital*

18

was published, and in the same year the book *Concerning Criticism of the Political Economy* was printed. Friedrich Engels corrected and edited the second (1885) and third (1894) part of *Capital* after Marx's death.

KARL MARX AND THE INTERNATIONAL LABORERS ASSOCIATION

Delegations of laborers from many capitalistic countries attended the London trade fair in 1862. In 1863 a riot of laborers in Poland was brutally suppressed, and this caused great agitation in other countries. On September 28, 1864, delegations from France, Germany, Poland, and Italy met at St. Martin's Hall in London. Here the "International Laborers Association" (First International) was founded. Marx devised the regulations and delivered the so-called "Inaugural Address," in which the following points were considered:

a) The emancipation of the working classes must be reached by the classes themselves. The war for the emancipation of the laborer class is not a fight for class privileges and monopolies but for equal rights and obligations; this means the abolition of every rule of classes.

b) The economic dependence of laborers on the owner of the means of labor as the source of livelihood forms the basis of slavery in every form and the basis of social misery, mental and spiritual atrophy, and practical dependence. Thus the great aim is economic emancipation, in which every political movement serves as a means of support.

c) All efforts directed to this great aim had failed previously because of the lack of unity among the many branches of labor in every country and because of the lack of cooperation between the working classes of the different lands.

d) The emancipation of labor is neither a local nor a national problem but a social one which embraces all those countries in which modern society exists. The solution of this problem depends on the practical and theoretical cooperation of most of the developed countries.

e) The present revival of the working classes in the industrial countries of Europe, while awakening new hopes, solemnly warns against a return to old wrong ways and requires the immediate alliance of all the movements now separated.

Therefore the International Laborers Association declares that it and all organizations and individuals belonging to it acknowledge truth, right, and morality as the basis of their relations to each other and to all fellow beings without distinctions of color, confession, or nationality. The International Laborers Association considers itself obligated to demand the rights of a man and citizen not only for itself but also for everybody who fulfills his duties: no duties without rights, and no rights without duties!

Marx stated that the technical evolution of industry produced a further separation of laborers and owners, which intensified the social conflict. For Marx the gain of the 10-hour day for the English laborer was a victory of the principle. The law of supply and demand no longer ruled, but the principle of the workers' class became effective: the rule over production by social insight and attention. The cooperative movement demonstrated that the abolition of wagework was possible. If this was to effect more than the correction of an entirely wrong system of capitalistic competition, then the political power of the workers would have to be established with the aim of ruling over the state. Therefore again: "Proletarians of all countries — unite!" (According to W. Banning, *Karl Marx . . . ,* p. 44 ff.)

Marx asserted himself against a vehement opposition, for the different delegations of the many countries differed from each other in their concepts, especially from the French followers of Proudhon, or the group of the anarchist Bakunin, which consisted of revolutionaries whose aim was revolution as a precondition for the freedom of mankind, in the sense of a brutal destruction of everything existing. There were many delegates who voted for truth, right, and morality, but did not consider realistically the real economic relations of power which were of central importance to Marx.

Even sharper contrasts could be observed at the next congress in Basel, Switzerland, in 1869. The national feelings on every side caused by the war between Germany and France in 1870 interrupted all contacts. Paris suffered the riot of the "Commune" in March 1871; in it the ideas of Bakunin and Proudhon were authoritative. The riot was defeated. Marx analysed the events in his "Address on the Civil War in France of 1871." The defeat of the "Commune" was the fate of the I.L.A., too. The congress of the Hague, Netherlands, in 1872 voted for the transfer of headquarters to New York, but the organization was no longer important.

Marx's mission came to an end after the First International collapsed. No new concepts were added to his previous ideas. In 1873 he suffered a physical breakdown. His wife passed away from cancer in 1881, and he himself died on March 13, 1883.

Six years later, the Second International was founded (1889).

Chapter 2

Marxist Doctrines

Scholars of Marxism differentiate several periods in the development of Karl Marx's thoughts. We have to take this into consideration, although our primary interest is not a historical review of that ideology. The principles of the system were developed by Marx (and Engels) by 1845-46, when its theories were spelled out in the "German Ideology." The *Communist Manifesto* of February 1848 can be judged as the thetic expression of the results. This shall, therefore, be used as the chief basis of our presentation. Although in later times Marx was expecially engaged with economic problems, our main concern is the explanation of Marx's understanding of anthropology and religion (Christianity).

ANTHROPOLOGY

Marx's understanding of man is imbedded in Feuerbach's anthropological thought. Feuerbach taught that the adoration of God, revelation, and faith are not realities outside man but products created by him, and projections of his longings and unrealizable wishes; namely, they were illusions. This philosopher represented a radical atheism and a radical humanism (such as the idea of natural egotism—seeing the impulse for happiness in man's nature as opposed to Hegel's idealistic "spirit"). Atheism and humanism should be viewed as a concentration of things on this side, that is, on our earthly lives. Man has to be considered as a kind or sort (*Gattungswesen*, a "natural being"). Truth is only what is real; truth, reality, and sensuality or material existence are the same. Man needs sensually recognizable things and beings; he does not live by abstract, metaphysical, and theological imaginations.

Marxism as a unique system begins with a radical turn to real life on this earth. In his time this was identified with atheism. In defining man, Marx spoke of the dialectical identity of his essence with nature: nature is man's object and product, and man is nature's object and product. Matter is necessary for man (1) as the object of his labor (and thus of his education, of his history, and of his own humanity), and (2) as the object which provides for his physical preservation. To this extent nature is man's further "inorganic body."

Christianity has to be considered the enemy of every true anthropology, for it separates body and soul, flesh and spirit (cf. John 6:63).

21

Because of this dualism it is concerned only with the abstract man, the "soul," while Marx asked for the empirical man. Christianity not only negates nature but devalues it and therefore destroys the nature-man relationship. The bourgeois society in its corrupted state today could only come into existence under Christianity. For since the natural relationship of the genus (*Gattung*) will dissolve and be replaced by an egotism seeking Christian salvation, nothing will hinder the dissolution of mankind into groups which face each other in enmity. (At this point the well-known sociologist Max Weber, who was a qualified admirer of Marx, tried to confront him with his theory of the genesis of the "spirit of capitalism" through the influence of ascetic Christian denominations like Calvinism and Pietism, etc.; cf. his *Protestant Ethics*.)

However, without the power of full material existence (*Sinnlichkeit*, according to the understanding of Marx's times) man is emasculated. The destruction of man's identity with nature consequently means the destruction of his own nature, because he becomes separated from the nature which is inherent in him and his own body. Christianity with her consciousness of sin virtually assassinates man, because only the soul is important for Christian dualism. The Christian, therefore, hopes for real life only after his death, according to Marxism.

Marx gives a clear "yes" to man's material existence. Human existence is a natural state with manifold needs. Hunger is typical for him. Sensual acquisition of an object is a necessity. Human labor originates in the drive for this object. This passion is called a real ontological determinism in Marx's system. However, his anthropology cannot be understood as a static definition of attributes of the human essence; rather, it has to be comprehended in a dialectical way. Man's existence is an action, that is, a relationship to an object permanently in motion—otherwise he is no longer a human being.

Man is always fluctuating between acquisition and disposition. He exists in a process and stands in a permanent evolution. Thus his senses change with their objects, and the objects change with man's disposition. This fact is already evident in man's identity with nature, which must be understood as a reciprocal process: man's identification with nature and nature's identification with man.

Man is in essence a social being, for he seeks himself in another being. The other person is the real object of natural human sensuality and passion. And love is the prototype of the process of dialectical identity. The relation between male and female is the origin of social relations. Klaus Bockmühl states: "Material existence is defined as the management of community and as determined by community: Material existence as preserved in community." This becomes true as an act, namely, as an event of history.

The contradiction between man and nature, between individuality and universality, is finally dissolved in sexual love. Marx said: "Society is man's perfect essential unity with nature, the true resurrection of nature, the accomplished naturalism of man and the accomplished humanism of nature" (Karl Marx, *Fruehschriften*, Kroener 237). Thus nature reaches its destination in socialism, in the human community. Mankind evolves toward this aim. (In his earlier writings Marx had spoken of "rough" Communism as the first stadium of the new society, and of socialism as the second; he later reversed this terminology. We also will use the latter, because it is the accepted one today.)

The individual remains a real individual inside the community. Individuality and universality are only extreme parts of the same essence, for man's essence is the totality of human beings as individuals. The dialectical identity of individual and collective man, according to Bockmühl, indicates an ambivalence which is characteristic of every dialectical identity. In Marx's later evolution the accent moved in favor of the collective.

Man has to be considered a synthesis of consciousness and being — of man and environment. Accordingly it is not permissible to ask whether consciousness is determined by being. But further evolution leads — especially through Engels' influence — to a deterministic understanding.

Human existence must be understood not only as a reciprocal movement between man and nature but also as an evolution. "Anthropology means history of nature and not only an ontological dialectical relationship" (Bockmühl). History is man's act of origination and his process of education. Man's genesis is to be described as a *generatio aequivoca*, because he is a product of the self-differentiation of nature. It is hopeless to infer from a causative series back to its origin, for the law of dialectical identity in history excludes the question of whether the hen or the egg came first. Erich Thier is correct when he states that Marx's assertion of an original generation of man cannot be proved by his system; it is a belief which will serve to save the totally secular character of his theory. Marx judged that man was not independent as long as he denied his essence as being subject to all things by believing in a creator.

The present history is defined as man's prehistory, because man is still living in the stage of alienation. This prehistory, however, can also be viewed as man's history, because it leads him to his essential being. When alienation is overcome in the socialist society, real history begins. This does not mean the end of dialectics or process, but the end of the period of serious contradiction as a hostile conflict.

"Alienation" is a term which Marx adopted from Hegel but transformed from idealistic philosophy into realism. The conditions of alienation and its abolition are reduced to the real process of production: Self-alienation is the consequence of conditions inside the process of production ruled by property, that is, by the power of money. This power alienates man from his real being.

The proletariat and the possessing class are opposites, but they do form a whole. Both are subjected in different ways to the same human self-alienation. In the proletariat, alienation comes into being because man loses his relationship to the product of his labor. First, progressive division of labor forces him to act in only a part of the process, with the result that the end-product is no longer in his visual field and responsibility. Second, man becomes alienated from nature because he has to live in the overcrowded workers' districts of the modern industrial towns. Third, the laborer in the capitalistic system is forced into submission. Fourth, the laborer has to sell his working power, his human power, in order to exist. On the employment market he is demoted to a ware (a commodity) which is of value only insofar as he is productive. Fifth, man is alienated from his neighbors, because the working process is no longer undertaken for the satisfaction of his needs of life but for profit, that is, for money. Sixth, the values of life are alienated. Economy and morality are entirely separated in capitalism, and a deterministic automatism rules. Finally, when the work is done only for wages, man alienates himself from his neighbor, and a new relation of master and slave comes into being. The possessing class also suffers alienation, although in another manner. It too exists under the power of money, which alienates man as a genus. Money is the alienating possession of mankind.

Thus, from the psychological point of view alienation is rooted in man's greediness. From the sociological point of view alienation results from the capitalist system. Accordingly, alienation will only be abolished when capitalism is removed by Communism. Communism means the liberation of mankind for a truly human existence.

In his earlier writings Marx mentioned that man's alienation was a necessary period, because it created necessary conditions non-existent during man's primitive period. Religion, state, and family brought forth the riches of the human essence; theology, for example, created the multitude of anthropological predicates in abstraction. Now man has to be liberated from alienation in order to become the true possessor of the goods thus brought into existence. This process can only be successful when for a time man is forced to live in a collective in which he has to renounce his individuality in order to win back his essential freedom.

In comparing Marx's anthropology with Christian anthropology we observe that his picture of Christianity is gained under specific circumstances. The attacked dualism can be considered idealism, understood as being in congruence with Christian convictions. Marx did not try to examine the real basis of Christianity, the Holy Scriptures, but used as arguments against Christian belief whatever he could find. His image of Christianity was often adopted from adversaries of this belief. Thus he used caricatures as found in Feuerbach, Bruno Bauer and his friends, David Friedrich Strauss, and others.

It would, however, be an illusion to assume that Marx would have argued differently if he had known Christianity better. He grew up under the influence of the era of Enlightenment (his father-in-law, Baron Ludwig von Westphalen, educated him in this way), and therefore it was self-evident to him that human reason was the only source and means of cognition about man, the world, and existence. Feuerbach's theory (that religion is nothing else than a projection of human wishes and longings unto heaven) supplied the bridge for Marx's exclusively secular anthropology.

Some of today's Marxist philosophers do not reject religion so strongly. Ernst Bloch asserts that man's self-alienation has deeper roots than those which can be explained simply by a wrongly structured society. He thinks that the concept of heaven is now almost meaningless, although it still has some content which must not be lost. This content is necessary even for the atheist, as long as he wants to keep his tendencies and aims. Religions are shells of a content which is now dead but was living in former times. Marxism should not ignore but should try to win back this very core. Bloch's kind of philosophy is an interesting development. It cannot be identified with Marx nor with materialistic ideology as preserved by true Communist Marxism in East and West.

We further know that Marx was enthusiastic over Darwin's theories of evolution. These are based on the idea that it is possible to prove a causal progression from the beginning of the kosmos until the period when man comes into being. Darwin's thoughts later were accepted as basic doctrine in Marxism. They demonstrate that Marxism felt the deficiency in its founder's arguments, in which a creation of the kosmos was neither assumed nor permitted. The negation of this is more important than the question, which position can be put against it: whether it is Marx's understanding of dialectical identity or Darwin's utopism. The main thing is that *belief* of any kind has no place inside the materialistic system. On the contrary, the system strongly asserts that it is based upon scientific truth only.

The phenomenon Bloch shows is that the longer it exists the less is Marxist anthropology able to prove itself as realistic. The new socialist societies were unable to abolish either religion or Christianity — even by the most brutal oppression. And the newest developments in

25

the natural sciences are beginning to turn away from Darwin's evolutionism.

The whole differentiation between a world on this side and one beyond, an immanent and a transcendent world, was brought up in the 17th century. It had its roots in the theological compendiums which since the times of Georg Calixt pretended that man was a subject within creation. This interpretation led by degrees to a banishment of God into the transcendent, while man was considered to be the very center of the world. The secular and the beyond were turned against each other.

Theology tried to provide a connection between the two worlds, while (atheistic) philosophy was eager to separate both from each other, and finally it denied the reality of God's transcendency. This attempt to expel God from His creation is fiction and does not accept the fact that the whole being is one and that God, the only and real *subiectum* of every being, can in no way be eliminated from it. Neither is God an *obiectum* opposite man on the same level, nor is He and the Godly area a projection of man's wishes, as Feuerbach and Marx, caught in the human self-understanding of their times, argued. This polarization of the whole into transcendency and immanence, to express the basic difference between God and man, is misused whenever those terms are used in an absolute manner.

We can observe a similar mistake in the supposed Christian separation of flesh and soul. The New Testament term *sarx* (flesh) stands not only for the material or natural side of a human being, but also for man as a being corrupted by sin, and who is therefore transitory. However, the differentiation should not be made between man's flesh and man's soul or spirit, but rather between God's Spirit and man's flesh, soul, and spirit. Man as a whole is sinful and therefore under God's wrath; and the whole man, not only his soul or spirit, needs to be saved. Idealism devalued man's physical part and overestimated his *ratio* (reason), and correspondingly his soul or spirit.

Such an understanding of Christian anthropology supported the evolution of capitalism and its social structures, against which Marxism was fighting. Those structures seemed to be legitimized by Christianity, for the official churches with very few exceptions ignored the roots of social miseries and with a good conscience made compacts with feudalism and capitalism.

Jesus did not try to change the social structures of His times on earth for the better, because He came in order to redeem mankind to His Father through His suffering and death on the cross; but His sermons against the egotism of wealthy and powerful people cannot be ignored. St. Paul could ask the slave Onesimus to be subject again to his master Philemon, but it finally was Christianity which destroyed

26

the slavery of Hellenistic times by setting examples of life and love.

The whole situation was changed within European Christianity in the 18th and 19th centuries. Here the church herself was considered to be a secular power, too, and she ruled according to her gained position. She often misunderstood Christ's word (that His kingdom is not of this world) and concluded that peoples' conditions in life were not at all relevant.

It is not possible to identify man with nature, as Marx does. His differentiation does not have a qualitative character; man is the highest natural development among all living beings but no more. It is wrong to say that only this kind of naturalism can open the way for man's true humanity. Man's real humanity is exclusively founded in his dependence on God and His will. Otherwise he misuses his neighbor and nature — as is finally evident even in Communist societies. Man, created in God's own image, has not become an ethically neutral being even after having lost this image, but he is always perverting nature and society without concern for his permanent responsibility to his Creator. Man's humanity is not based upon himself or upon nature but is only possible in obedience to his Lord.

This raises the question of ethical concerns in Marx's anthropology. He bases his picture of man on the process of dialectical identity. Relations between man and nature are good as long as man is not forced to live under adverse social conditions. Man is good, because his essence can only be comprehended in his relationship to nature and in the relationship of nature to man.

This tendency in Marx's system seems to be affected by ethics. The main accent lies on man as a social being. It is also difficult to consider the term "self-alienation" a synonym for the Christian word "sin." Marx says only that alienation is dependent on perverted social conditions, chiefly capitalism and its adoration of private property. Its abolition will correct human society. This alienation is further seen as a necessary factor in man's prehistory, for it developed his manifold possibilities as brought forth in religion, state, family, etc.

In other words the real history of man begins with the jump to socialist society. He is now still living in the prehistorical age, in which alienation is a typical feature of man's existence. This theory can hardly be compared to Christian ethics. Morality became strongly connected with the Marxist ideology itself and then with Communist nationalism, as is the case in Soviet Russia, Red China, etc. Here we even observe confessions of faults performed against (the current interpretation of) the ideology or against the state and government. At this point we need to ask whether Marxism cannot be considered a pseudoreligion, in which man stands as the ideal and idol which everything has to serve.

Christian ethics, on the contrary, is rooted in man's personal relationship to God. It is important to recognize that His will is voluntarily done by the saved being, that is, the Christian who trusts in his Savior. His decisions and actions therefore have an evangelical basis, and they are performed in love to God and thus to the neighbor and other beings. The danger of perversion grows when Christian congregations and synods become aware of their power as institutions. The consequence could be an over-emphasis on constitutions and orders to the eventual loss of the means of grace. A further consequence could be the attempt to use political means, as was demonstrated in the Inquisition and the Crusades.

According to God's revelation sin is not bound to certain social structures. That man is a sinner means that everything is under God's curse. There is no sinless relationship between man and nature, man and neighbor, but everything is infected with the same perversion. It is hopeless to attempt to change this situation by changing social or other secular structures or by abolishing private property.

CLASS CONFLICT AND SOCIETY

"The history of all hitherto existing society is the history of class struggles" — this sentence stands at the beginning of the first chapter of the *Communist Manifesto* (p. 57), and the following essay tries to prove that statement historically. Society consists of two groups: the oppressors and the oppressed. There was a manifold gradation in former societies, but since the bourgeois class took over the dominant role in the French Revolution, class antagonism was simplified. Only two classes stand against each other: bourgeoisie and proletariat.

> The bourgeoisie, wherever it has got the upper hand, has put an end to all feudal, patriarchal, idyllic relations. It has pitilessly torn asunder the motley feudal ties that bound man to his "natural superiors" and has left remaining no other bond between man and man than naked self-interest and callous "cash payment." It has drowned the most heavenly ecstasies of religious fervor, of chivalrous enthusiasm, of philistine sentimentalism, in the icy water of egotistical calculation. It has resolved personal worth into exchange value, and in place of the numberless indefeasible chartered freedoms, has set up that single, unconscionable freedom — free trade. In a word, for exploitation veiled by religious and political illusions, it has substituted naked, shameless, direct, brutal exploitation. (P. 61 f.)

The bourgeoisie can only exist by permanently revolutionizing the instruments of production, and thereby also the conditions of production. Through its exploiting dynamic it has given the world market a cosmopolitan production and consumption in every country. By the rapid improvement of all instruments of production and by the im-

28

mensely facilitated means of communication, it draws all nations — even the backward ones — into civilization. It has put the rural areas under the rule of the cities.

> The bourgeoisie is more and more doing away with the scattered state of the population, of the means of production, and of property. It has agglomerated population, centralized means of production, and has concentrated property in a few hands. The necessary consequence of this was political centralization. . . .

> The bourgeoisie, during its rule of scarcely one hundred years, has created more massive and more colossal productive forces than have all preceding generations together. (P. 65)

The means of production and exchange were generated in feudal society. At a certain stage of development the conditions of this society "became no longer compatible with the already developed productive forces . . . They had to be burst asunder; they were burst asunder." Free competition accompanied by the respective social and political constitution stepped in to replace those conditions. This was done with the economic and political influence of the bourgeois class.

This short summary of the first pages of the *Communist Manifesto* shows some important features of the Marxist view of society. It is always ruled by the development of production and property. Whenever social conditions fall behind the permanently developing means of production and exchange, a real change is necessary. Every historical event or period and every social structure and change can be explained on this economic basis; every other explanation is condemned as being an ideological and/or unscientific one.

The materialistic basis is evident. It originally was made a fact by the bourgeoisie, for this class destroyed every illusion and mythical justification of the dominating rights of a ruling class. The power of the bourgeois class is based upon its possession of the means of production and its use of them in a brutal way to enslave the other classes and to hold its own ground.

The *Communist Manifesto* continues by asserting that the development of society has again reached a critical stage:

> For many decades now the history of industry and commerce has been but the history of the revolt of modern productive forces against modern conditions of production, against the property relations that are the conditions for the existence of the bourgeoisie and of its rule. (P. 67)

The epidemic of overproduction is typical for that contemporary stadium. Society chokes on its own civilization, means of subsistence, industry, and commerce, for it has too many of them. The bourgeoisie has thus forged the weapons which in former times were used to overcome feudalism and are now killing it. It also brought into being the men who will wield those weapons, namely, the modern proletarian.

Which condition brings forth the new social crisis? The *Communist Manifesto* answers:

> Hitherto, every form of society has been based, as we have already seen, on the antagonism of oppressing and oppressed classes. But in order to oppress a class, certain conditions must be assured to it under which it can, at least, continue its slavish existence. The serf, in the period of serfdom, raised himself to membership in the commune, just as the petty bourgeois, under the yoke of feudal absolutism, managed to develop into a bourgeois. The modern laborer, on the contrary, instead of rising with the progress of industry, sinks deeper and deeper below the conditions of existence of his own class. He becomes a pauper, and pauperism develops more rapidly than population and wealth. And here it becomes evident that the bourgeoisie is unfit any longer to be the ruling class in society, and to impose its conditions of existence upon society as an overriding law. It is unfit to rule because it is incompetent to assure an existence to the slave within its slavery — because it cannot help letting him sink into such a state, that it has to feed him, instead of being fed by him. Society can no longer live under this bourgeoisie, in other words, its existence is no longer compatible with society. (P. 77 f.)

The laborers become a ware (a commodity) under the social conditions created by the bourgeoisie. They have to sell themselves, that is, their working power, and are therefore exposed to all the vicissitudes of competition and to all the fluctuations of the market. They find work as long as their labor increases capital (capital will be spoken of from now on as a synonym for the bourgeoisie in the *Communist Manifesto*). The extensive use of machinery and the division of labor in the bourgeois industrial working process alienate the proletarians, for their work loses its individual character, and consequently all its charms for the workman. The cost of production is restricted entirely to the means of subsistence that the laborer requires for his maintenance and for the propagation of his race. The laborer is not only enslaved by his inspector in the plant but also by the machine.

> The more openly this despotism proclaims gain to be its end and aim, the more petty, the more hateful, and the more embittering it becomes. (P. 70)

The less skill and strength are demanded in the manual labor of modern industry, the more may the labor of men be superseded by that of women. The differences of age and sex are cancelled, for everybody is only considered an instrument of labor. After the exploitation by the manufacturer is finished and the wages are paid the worker in cash, he is then set upon by the landlord, the shopkeeper, the pawn-broker, etc.

Strong competition kills the lower middle classes, and they finally all join the proletariat. Thus there are only two classes: the bourgeoisie and the proletariat.

Still, opposition to the ruling conditions of life is growing. Working men gather into unions and defend their existence in local areas. They destroy the instruments of production and the factories. The unification of proprietors against those gatherings brings forth wider labor associations. The really effective organization of the proletariat, however, is provided by the Communists, who have only one aim: the abolition of (bourgeois) private property, which is the root of all evils. Their program is described as follows:

1. Abolition of property in land and application of all rents of land to public purposes.
2. A heavy progressive or graduated income tax.
3. Abolition of all right of inheritance.
4. Confiscation of the property of all emigrants and rebels.
5. Centralization of credit in the hands of the state, by means of a national bank with state capital and an exclusive monopoly.
6. Centralization of the means of communication and transport in the hands of the state.
7. Extension of factories and instruments of production owned by the state; the bringing into cultivation of wastelands, and the improvement of the soil generally in accordance with a common plan.
8. Equal liability of all to labor. Establishment of industrial armies, especially for agriculture.
9. Combination of agriculture with manufacturing industries; gradual abolition of the distinction between town and country, by a more equable distribution of the population over the country.
10. Free education for all children in public schools. Abolition of children's factory labor in its present form. Combination of education with industrial production, etc., etc. (P. 94)

Looking at such a program we may ask whether it does not plainly propose what later on became the reality in the eastern Communist countries. Every power and authority is given to the state, and the slavery continues under the structure of state capitalism as declared above. However this was not the intention of the *Communist Manifesto*. For the state ought to play another role in future Communist society

31

than that of bourgeoisie. Class conflict is finished when the proletarian revolution is performed and every other social class is destroyed. The remaining proletariat and the state are one. Society has jumped into an entirely new period of existence.

> In place of the old bourgeois society, with its classes and class antagonisms, we shall have an association in which the free development of each is the condition for the free development of all. (P. 95)

When we see the states which are structured according to Marxism, the utopian character of the whole program becomes evident. The socialist revolution and the expropriation of private property has removed neither the class system nor the slavery of the workers. Already Marx and Engels spoke of the two periods in the development of society after the revolution took place. The first step was to be the so-called "socialist society." It must be viewed as a transition period, while the "Communist society" would be the final aim. The difference between these two stages is as follows: The first one would be the dictatorship of the proletariat in which men would have to be paid according to their workmanship ("From everybody according to his capacities; to everybody according to his pieces of work").

Later on the classless or "Communist society" would have the formula: "From everybody according to his capacities; to everybody according to his needs." But it was not intended that the first stage should endure almost five and a half decades, as is the fact with Russian socialism. On the contrary, the rise of another social structure may be observed, which has already stagnated and may, therefore, be judged as a traditional order in the dictatorship of the proletariat. All those phenomena cannot be explained simply by the fact that Russian society at the beginning of our century was not of that type imagined by Marx, but was to an overwhelming extent stamped by small farmers.

We cite two main reasons for the wrong analysis of society by Marxism: the absolutely materialistic comprehension as already noted in Marx's anthropology; and an antibourgeois complex, which dominates in the sketch of present and future society.

With respect to the second observation we note that the aims of the Communists are often defended by showing wrong developments within the bourgeoisie along the lines of: "You are no better than we are!" To furnish some examples from the Communist Manifesto:

> You are horrified at our intending to do away with private property. But in our existing society, private property is already done away with for nine-tenths of the population . . . You reproach us, therefore, with intending to do away with a form of property, the necessary condition for whose existence is the nonexistence of any property for the immense majority of society. (P. 85)

32

But, you say, we destroy the most hallowed of relations, when we displace home education by social.

And your education! Is it not also social and determined by the social conditions under which you educate, by the intervention, direct or indirect, of society by means of schools etc.? The Communists have not invented the intervention of society in education; they merely seek to alter the character of that intervention and to rescue education from the influence of the ruling class. (P. 88)

It is obvious that argumentation with the bourgeois adversary tries to show that Communism wants to legitimize what is already a real custom, especially in bourgeois society. The bourgeoisie fills the form of society with its egotistic contents, while the Communists fight to become rulers and use these means according to their wishes. They believe that the socialist revolution will sweep away every class structure in society, because only one class will survive: the proletariat.

Christianity cannot confirm the bourgeois practice which is attacked by Marxism. It has no mandate to form a compact with capitalism or with any other secular social structure in order to sanctify it. Christianity proclaims God's saving acts to sinful mankind, the social structures of which will always be perverted by sin. Christians will, according to their Lord's commandment, practice His love in every social constellation, whether it is divided into classes or is classless. Christianity knows that man's perversion is still effective in her own midst, that is, in her social structures of congregations and synods. The Gospel is not directed to structures but to man. When man's relationship with God can be corrected, then there is hope that this correction can affect even social orders for the better. Christian social activity is not social at all if it is understood in the secular meaning of the term as in Marxism. It is rather *diakonia* (service) as a reflection of God's love to people.

A real problem comes up in this regard, which can be described with the double question: Must Christianity cooperate with an ideology, when its social aims or at least some of them seem to be good? Or has she first of all to test its doctrinal basis in order to decide whether she can cooperate or not?

Today both questions are often answered positively: One group wants Christianity to be a partner of Communists in those areas which are stamped by pauperization as the consequence of an extreme capitalistic system; the other group wants Christianity to be a confederate in the struggle against Communist imperialism. Both groups cannot comprehend that Christianity is neither a political crusader against Marxism nor is it to be used as a political ally for the purpose of destroying certain secular structures. Christians have a God-given mandate which dare not be subjected by social systems and thus become incorporated into their secular aims.

This critical analysis of Marxism should not prevent Christianity from admitting that some ideas of that ideology sound good. Christianity is against slavery and would like to see everybody free from misery and social oppression. At the same time it is her conviction that freedom is impossible as long as there is no real responsibility to God. Man cannot solve his problems by himself; ignoring the Creator and man's own sin means that conditions will worsen, not improve.

Property in itself is not bad but the man who uses it may be. There is no difference; whether we speak of private possession or of state capitalism there is always a group or class which is privileged above others to own or to enjoy. Rich and poor people will always exist in society under God's permission—just as will more or less intelligent ones. The problem is whether everybody uses his gifts according to God's will or according to his selfishness. Classes in society are social structures even as monarchy or democracy are structures on the political level; the question is whether they are filled with responsibility to God and the neighbor or whether the structures are being used for the benefit of a certain group at the cost of the other members of society.

Marx rejected every responsibility to God and attacked every belief in the Creator; he was convinced that man can and must create his own conditions for living perfectly. Consequently the socialist revolution as pictured in his system can only create new wrong social structures. And the brutality of Marx's system, based totally upon his materialistic understanding of the law, could result in nothing but an increase of the slavery and misery for the majority and more favors for the new privileged class: the Communist party.

Marx asserted that the perverted society can be healed by the Communist abolition of private property, the most important cause of man's alienation. He adopted Proudhon's statement, "Property is larceny." But does this heavily emphasized slogan really fit into Marxist anthropology? His description of dialectical identity describes private property as "robbed" property. Man's hunger aims at the total acquisition of the wanted object. Love between male and female, the root of every social relation, is first of all defined in a materialistic way (the *Communist Manifesto*, p. 89 f.) and means the complete (sexual) possession of each other. Private property is the isolation of an object for one's use, and this can, under certain circumstances, include the proprietor's entire attitude toward it. This was the original basis of Marx's anthropology. His anthropology could, therefore, change the relations of property, but it was not able to replace property with a new value.

Even state capital has a private character to a certain extent, for the use of it is still a privilege of a class which by its power is able to lay claim to the fulfillment of needs on a higher level than the average laborer is permitted. Marx might have felt that problem and in earlier writings differentiated between private and individual property. The latter was tolerated. In later times the individual was replaced by the collective, and individual property was no longer spoken of.

HISTORICAL AND DIALECTICAL MATERIALISM

Marx's thoughts on historical materialism can best be studied in his work *Concerning Criticism of Political Economy* (1859). It is obvious that a dependence on Hegel's idealistic theory of historical dialectics exists—assimilated, however, into Marx's realism.

During the social production period of their lives people enter certain definite and necessary relations. These are independent of their wills and correspond to stages of development in their material productivity. All these relations of production together form the economic structure of society, upon which a legal and political superstructure rises. The economic structure has corresponding definite social forms of consciousness (*Bewusstseinsformen*). The manner of production in the material life shapes the whole social, political, and spiritual process of living. Man's consciousness does not coin his being, but vice versa, his social being moulds his consciousness. When a certain step in the evolution of mankind is reached, the material powers of production available in the society begin to contradict the productive conditions at hand with the very structures of property inside which they were previously functioning.

At this point the evolving structures of productivity become chains. This produces a period of social revolution which not only changes the economic basis of the society but also the immense superstructure based upon it. It is important in considering a revolution that one differentiate between the revolution inside the economic conditions of production and the ideological forms in which men become conscious of this conflict and fight it (law, politics, religion, art, philosophy). Only the materialistic revolution can be recognized as scientifically true.

As an individual can scarcely be judged according to what he thinks of himself, so a revolutionary period can scarcely be judged from its own consciousness. Rather it is necessary to explain the revolution by considering the contradictions in material life and the conflict between the social powers of productivity and the conditions of production. A social formation never perishes as long as all powers of production, for which this formation is good enough, are still developing. Higher conditions of production will never take their place before the material conditions sprout in the shoot of the old society. Therefore mankind can only set such tasks as it is able to solve.

For a task is only defined after the material conditions for its solution already exist or are at least in the process of appearing. The bourgeois conditions of production are the last antagonistic forms in the social process of production. (Marx understands antagonism as a state which arises out of the social conditions of individual lives.) The powers of production evolving from the shoot of the bourgeois society create the material conditions for the dissolution of this antagonism. The prehistory of human society will conclude with this last formation (socialism) of society.

Marx's historical materialism makes his dialectics evident. His "new materialism" does not express dialectics in formal-logical words (as was done by Hegel, according to the materialist philosophers) but in real contrasts in the area of the economic relations of power: the contrasts of classes. For although bourgeoisie and proletariat are contrasts, they form a whole. Both are structures in the world of private property. Both have a definite but contrasting stand. They are not two sides of a whole. Private possession as such is forced to preserve itself and thereby also preserve its contrast.

The positive side of the contrast is private property as satisfied in itself. In reverse the proletariat is forced to eliminate itself and thus its conditioned contrast, which makes it the proletariat, namely, private property. Tension will grow until the oppressed class will destroy the whole structure of society in order to eliminate the overstrained situation. Private property as the source and root of all (social) evils will be abolished. Marx did not consider his dialectics to be his individual interpretation of the world and its history but as the real situation which would occur, whether it was wanted or not.

It is evident that Marx's way of interpreting history is a very mechanistic one. Hegel still knows a "Weltvernunft" as the leading power in history; Marx replaces even that by the development of the powers and conditions of production. Hegel names consciousness of freedom as the final aim; Marx defines Communist society as the immediate aim. While Hegel speaks of a continuing process of history, Marx asserts that mankind is now living in the last period of prehistory, which is to be overcome by his socialist society.

The denial of the living God forced Marx to interpret everything legalistically. He was so convinced of the correctness of his materialistic ideas that he believed in them in spite of every experience of his lifetime. We know that, while no non-Communist nation in Western Europe voluntarily accepted the Marxist view until today, the socialist society was introduced by revolutions in areas which did not have Marx's social preconditions. Marxism was forced to correct and even to change its system in order to accommodate to the social conditions which changed in ways different from Marx's mechanistic prophecy.

36

The accumulative stage predicted by Marx never came. History moved in another direction.

We must nevertheless admit that Marx's system, based upon accurate observations, is intelligible to our reason and very attractive. Whenever Christians of our day are confronted with the abominable conditions in slums of Western capitalist societies and begin to study their origins, they will easily come to similar conclusions. They may find it very difficult to trust in a personal God who leads history and everybody in it, especially when miseries seem to remain for generations inside an unmovable social structure. Marx's – and Hegel's – law of necessary revolutions seems to be more humane than Christian patience, which refuses to upset wrong social structures by powerful revolution. Often no rationale for Christian acts of *diakonia* can be recognized, for they seem to be as effective as a small drop in the ocean.

Marx's historical materialism is valid as long as the revolution lies in the future. It is out of date once a revolution has taken place in a country and a dictatorship of the proletariat has been founded. The danger in connection with this idea is that it can be effective even after mankind has been able to leave the prehistoric stage and reach the historical one. It is, for example, a serious question as to whether the evolution of the powers and conditions of production in Communist countries are always matched to their socialist structures. If this is not the case, the new society stands in the danger of suffering a new antithesis and finally a new revolution, a fact which is in principle fully possible, according to Marx's basic thought.

We are not concerned here with whether the roots of dialectical materialism (DIAMAT) can be proven already in the first part of Marx's writings. (Bockmühl mentions his "German Ideology," part I; and W. Banning states that this basic doctrine or philosophy could only come into existence in Russia. Some theses are based upon natural science and its theory of evolutionism, a topic which was hardly considered by Marx.) It is evident, however, that this thought began to play an important role after Communism was victorious in Russia.

Lenin and his co-workers enlarged Marxism to a totalitarian conception of life and ideology, which since 1958 has been fixed in an official handbook. We find the following keypoints: Marxism consists of three parts, which are combined insolubly with each other: philosophy as a complete ideology; economy; and the theory of scientific socialism. The philosophical elements are historical and dialectical materialism as the ideology of the revolutionary working class and the Marxist party. In contrast to religion, this philosophy is based upon facts. It is a science, and it determines human action.

The basic question of philosophy – the problem of the relation between thinking and being, spirit and nature – is answered by the allocation of first place to the material, and therefore by the rejection of every kind of idealism and religion. This philosophy is to be described simply as a scientific method, not as a science, for it discloses only the connections and phenomena in the cosmos, nature, man, and society. It explains everything which comes into existence, every evolution and development. Accordingly, it is the method which normalizes everything.

Dialectical and historical materialism, however, is not only a science but a comprehensive guide, the spiritual weapon of the proletariat in its struggle for liberation. It frees the working class from the yoke of religion which in all its appearances is superstition. It also frees from capitalism, imperialism, and militarism. Thus the idea of revolution receives its theoretical basis in the areas of economy, sociology, and politics from the dialectical-materialistic explanation of natural laws.

A private view of life is no longer possible for the Communist. He has to be a materialist, for the party presents the philosophical characteristic features of Marxism as the conviction of the party. The party also is an infallible authority, an ideological monolith, so far as intellectuality is concerned. Only the reasoning of middle-class people can misunderstand this as force or as an attack against personal freedom. The dialectical-materialistic philosophy is scientific truth and therefore always objective and liberating, says Marxism.

Dialectical materialism is the basic doctrine of Eastern Marxism. Its starting point is matter in movement: everything exists in a process of permanent becoming and dying. This has to be comprehended as a dialectical evolution, that is, not as a gradual process but as a permanent struggle of contrasts, because the new can only come into existence by the destruction of the old. This dialectical movement originates in the material powers of the cosmos, which consist of nothing but the movable. All natural laws and phenomena are related to it. The term "movement" should not be understood mechanistically, because five different forms have to be distinguished:

1. The movement of bodies with regard to other bodies within a space
2. The forms of movement which belong to physics (thermal and electromagnetic phenomena)
3. Chemical phenomena
4. Biological forms of movement
5. Social developments, that is, the history of society inclusive of intellectual insights.

"Movement" is comprehended as absolute; it can, therefore, neither be destroyed nor created; it is relative (existing in passing phenomena only); it is dialectical (it takes place in contrasts, and therefore contains moments of continuity and discontinuity).

It is important to know that Eastern Marxism condemns other ways of thinking. DIAMAT is its absolute conviction and belief; its equation (dialectical materialism = science = absolute truth) hinders every fair discussion with other convictions and/or ideologies.

A certain similarity with the Christian understanding of dogma seems to exist at least in principle; every religion and pseudo-religion tries steadfastly to preserve its doctrines. This formal correspondence, however, is not enough for stating a similarity between Marxism and Christianity. The most extreme contrast is evident in the fact that the Triune God—the Creator of all things, the Savior, and the Sanctifier—is the essential center and aim of Biblical revelation and Christian belief; while a creation, namely matter in movement, is the only and very center of Marxism. Christianity confesses to be a belief which can only be found in God's grace; it does not want to rule the nations or society politically. (Historical misuse of the Gospel by churches and governments cannot disprove the clear New Testament statements in this regard. They are authoritative for all Christianity.)

Marxism claims to be no belief at all but science, capable of being tested every time, although not with "bourgeois means." Everybody must confess Marxism as the only truth. According to its principles no other ideology nor religion can be tolerated in its realm. Marxism is extremely political and demands to rule the whole man. While the Gospel of Christ is the life-giving power in Christianity, which culminates in love to God and neighbor, law and order is the energy in Marxism, pushing forward everybody in its realm. We conclude, therefore, that Marxist ideology and Christian belief are mutually exclusive opposites.

THE SUPERSTRUCTURE

Willem Banning remarks that a house, nice and beautiful as it might look with its facades and comfortable living-rooms, is always built upon its unlovely basement, and the inconspicuous kitchen plays a most important part for the family which lives there. A change of the foundation will change the whole building and influence its look decisively. This illustration can be applied when we try to understand the Marxist term "superstructure." The *Communist Manifesto* states:

> The proletariat, the lowest stratum of our present society, cannot raise itself up, without the whole superincumbent strata of official society being sprung into the air. (P. 77)

The proletariat has to destroy the present capitalistic social structures. This will only happen when it becomes independent of the spiritual conceptions of capitalism. The understanding of law, politics, religion, art, and philosophy is based upon the social structures of capitalism and receives its meaning from it. We remember Marx's statement in his "Criticism of Political Economy": "Man's consciousness does not coin his being, but social being moulds his consciousness. The relations of production form society, including its legal and political self-understanding. Social structures are not based upon religious, philosophical, and legal convictions but, conversely, religion, law, etc. are based upon existing social structures."

Marx's materialistic world view stands in real contradiction to Hegel's idealistic system. Everything belonging to the superstructure will automatically be destroyed with the change of its basis. The dominating class shapes the structures of the whole society, and therefore it forms the respective superstructure according to its self-interest. The oppressed classes will be enslaved by this superstructure since it is the effective instrument of the ruling class. Law, philosophy, religion, etc. are exercised in favor of the proprietors and of the bourgeoisie, while the proletariat can expect nothing from them except some empty illusions. Especially religion saps every energy of the oppressed, for it promises a better life in an invisible and unprovable beyond, thus directing the poor people's minds away from their daily hurtful existence.

Marx especially developed his criticism on religion in his work "Concerning Criticism on Hegel's Philosophy of Law" (1843). He said that man brings forth religion; religion does not produce man. Religion is man's self-consciousness and self-feeling, for either he has not yet gained his own self, or he has already lost himself again. But man is not an abstract being who squats outside the world. Man is man's world, state, and society. This state and society produce religion, and religion is a wrong consciousness of the world because it *is* a wrong world. Religion is the general theory of the world, its encyclopedic compendium, its logic in popular form, its spiritualistic *point d'honneur*, its enthusiasm, its moral sanction, its solemn completion, its comprehensive reason for comfort, and its justification. Religion is the fantastic realization of the human being who does not own free reality. The fight against religion is, therefore, the immediate struggle against a world of which the spiritual flower is religion. Religious misery is on one side the expression of real misery and on the other side a protest against real misery. Religion is the sigh of the oppressed creature, the mind of a heartless world, and the spirit of spiritless conditions. Religion is the opium of the people. (Lenin changed this sentence in 1905 to: ". . . for the people." For sources of the use of the term "opium" in relation to Marxism, see Helmut Gollwitzer, *Die marxistische Religionskritik und der christliche Glaube*, p. 23 ff.)

40

The demand for real happiness abolishes religion as the illusory happiness of the people. Criticism of religion is, therefore, in its beginning the criticism of this vale of tears, the aureola of which is religion. It is the task of history to establish the truth of the world on this side, after the beyond of the truth is gone. It is also the task of philosophy, which serves history in unmasking self-alienation in its nonholy forms. Herewith the criticism of heaven changes to a criticism of earth; criticism of religion changes into a criticism of law; criticism of religion changes into the criticism of politics. (Cf. Kroener, p. 207 ff.)

The following paragraphs in the *Communist Manifesto* can now be understood in their whole context:

> Undoubtedly it will be said, religious, moral, philosophical, and juridical ideas have been modified in the course of historical development. But religion, morality, philosophy, political science, and law constantly survived this change.
>
> There are, besides, eternal truths such as freedom, justice, etc., that are common to all states of society. But communism abolishes eternal truths, it abolishes all religion and all morality, instead of constituting them on a new basis; it therefore acts in contradiction to all past historical experience. (P. 92)

These words illustrate anew the strong conviction of its adherents that Marxism will be able to lead mankind into an entirely new period in its evolution.

Marx's description is as fascinating as it is wrong. It is fascinating because many people have experienced manipulation by religion, just as Marx described. This misuse of Christian beliefs can easily lead one to ask whether God as preached in the churches might be a tool in the hands of individuals who want to protect their privileges. A silent Christianity, which not only ignores social oppression but tolerates it, even inside her own parishes and synodical institutions, gives support to such a way of thinking. We cannot deny that the atheistic doctrines of Marxism first became meaningful among oppressed classes in societies which had been marked by Christianity for centuries.

Another question arises: how is it with pagan religions? Do they not picture their god(s) according to man's own being and his societies? Friedrich von Schiller seems to be correct when he writes: "Man paints himself in his gods." There is a line which goes from man to religion. May this not also be true with regard to man's ethics, etc.?

It is a surprising fact that Communist governments were not able to abolish or to expel religion—especially Christianity—in their areas. This is not only true for those groups which are still brutally enslaved under socialism. Many individuals—scientists, engineers, and businessmen—are still religiously minded and even Christian, although they enjoy the privileges of their societies. Every effort made to overcome religiosity scientifically did not achieve the desired result. Sharp laws and brutal punishments could push Christianity underground but not destroy her. These facts are what may have led Marxist philosophers like Ernst Bloch and others to ask whether the phenomenon of religion is fully explained with Marx's reconstruction.

In opposing Christian belief based upon Holy Scripture to Marx's system of basis and superstructure, we state that religiousness originates in man's conscience. There is a residual knowledge that God exists and that man is responsible to Him. This knowledge is hardly more than the presentiment that there is something or somebody above man to which he is subjected. It can, therefore, evolve in many ways (as monotheism or pantheism) and with many different orders and cultic rites. These many phenomena are called religions. It cannot be contested that these religions connect man's knowledge of something above him (God) and of human values and experiences during his life, and project them to heaven in a most ideal form. But man's misery as such does not force him to establish religion; rather, the God-given presentiment in his conscience leads him to do so.

Christianity is not a religion in the sense of man's projection of his own ideals and wishes to heaven, based upon the presentiment of a god in his conscience. Christianity is in all facets, even to the most specific details, revealed by the true God Himself. Faith in the Christian God is, therefore, not based upon the attempt to flee this world and its bad (social) conditions. Rather, it is the Lord's gift and is brought about only by Him in man's heart.

God revealed His will and grace in human form, pictures, and illustrations. More than that, His Son became flesh, a human being, and lived among us in order to save us from death and condemnation. God's condescension, however, does not mean that His acts for our salvation can be understood by human reason. They remain unbelievable as far as our ability to comprehend them is concerned. With my own reason I am only able to reject His work. It makes no difference whether I am rich or poor, intelligent or stupid, young or old, healthy or sick. The moment I transform God's revealed will and deeds into terms which I can understand, the moment I change not only their formal character but also their content, I change Christianity into mere religion. Then my belief in it is not God's gift but a product of reason which I am able to explain and for which I can make my decisions.

Because of sin, man's consciousness stands with the different structures of society under God's curse. Whether man's being coins his consciousness or vice versa is a secondary problem. Therefore the whole theory of basis and superstructure does not deal with man's reality, which cannot be truly analysed apart from our Creator and

Lord. This is recognized by Lenin, too, when he asserts that only the Communist party is able and should be allowed to interpret the whole ideology, while middle-class people will invariably misunderstand this as a use of force or as an attack against personal freedom. Thus Communism becomes an unprovable doctrine, that is, provable only after one accepts the preconditioned methods of thinking demanded by the party.

God's curse does not mean that the Creator has turned away from His world after the fall of man into sin. He is still preserving and ruling His creation, including man. His will is effective and appears to a certain extent in human law. His orders of preservation cannot be permanently eliminated in man's existence, or man will finally destory himself. Marx's materialistic understanding of love, for example, could not in its totality be supported in Soviet Russia, but the order of marriage and family did gain a new value.

Marxism does not take this whole theory of basis and superstructure as seriously as asserted. Instead of doing away with the state and its government, the parties evolved a strong nationalism which created a heavy burden for the unity of world Communism. Dialectical materialism, the basis of which lies in systems typical of bourgeois philosophy, is the dominating philosophy. The superstructure of Marxism's socialist society, therefore, possesses indissoluble connections with the superstructure of the "overcome" bourgeois society. Darwin, Feuerbach, and others were not Communist, and we can show that the positive descriptions of the future Communist society developed by Engels were mainly adopted from other socialist groups which were sharply attacked and condemned (for example, in the *Communist Manifesto* p. 96 ff.; look especially at Marx's polemics against Proudhon, p. 107, whose assertion "Property is larceny," was adopted as an important slogan of Communism).

It should be said that a materialistic world view has grown up in the western hemisphere, independent of Marxism; for example, modern practical atheism, which has produced an extremely materialistic understanding of man. Sexuality, ethics, human order, etc. are founded upon an anthropological basis which lacks all social responsibility. This raises the question of whether Marxism is an ideology stamped only with the economico-philosophical thoughts of its founder, and therefore simply one possible development among others.

What is called "nihilism" in Western thought shows the same basic convictions, except that it is not formulated within a system of pseudo-religious character. This decadent materialistic attitude, by the way, also dominates the majority of the population inside Communist countries. This means that Communism and Christianity are both minorities in countries where the overwhelming majority of the population has no ideological or religious convictions at all.

We conclude that it is not possible to eliminate the atheistic element from Marx's ideology without destroying the whole system. Materialism and Christianity exclude each other; this is also true when no specifically Marxist materialism is involved. The dialectical materialism of Communism, however, possesses a strong pseudo-religious character, which negates every tolerance for another ideology or religion. Marxism would destroy itself if it were willing to remove its atheistic basis. It would then no longer be Marxism.

THE SECULARIZED ESCHATOLOGY OF MARXISM

Communism purports to mean the liberation of mankind for true human existence. This ideology, therefore, is an aim or a hope. Socialist society is to be a perfect social structure. All economic problems are to be solved. Economy is to be understood as the basis of man's life. When this basis is right, then the superstructure will be good, too. Fulfilled humanity will rule on earth. Communism seeks heaven on earth. The world is changed into a paradise. Alienation is destroyed, and man's reintegration takes place. Engels' statement will be a reality: "From everybody according to his capacities; to everybody according to his needs" — needs which are, of course, on the same level for everybody.

Engels wrote in his brochure *The Development of Socialism from Utopia to Science* (1882):

> The socialization and the planned, deliberate organization of production make man a real ruler of society the same as he has already subdued nature. This is the leap of mankind from the realm of necessity into the realm of freedom. The period of prehistory, in which class conflicts were dominant, is finished. The real history of free mankind will begin.

This statement sounds like a confession of hope, and we recall some of the earlier statements of Marx which contained the same belief.

There seems to be a striking parallel to Christian eschatology. Marxism speaks of an integral human being, who was lost because of self-disunion and self-alienation as a consequence of the ruling social conditions. The healing of the loss lies in the classless society of the future. Thus Marxism acquires a salvatory character. It is a messianic message with a real hope. This and the assertion that it is the result of scientific research and cognition, gave Marxism the power which conquered parts of the world some decades later. At the beginning of the 20th century many poems and essays were published which described this expectation of Marxist salvation in religious terms. However, the message is deceptive; it creates a false security by teaching the reasonableness of its eschatological hope. Banning says:

44

[Marxism] appears in the European world, which as a bourgeoisie stands on the highest point with its mechanistic materialism as far as its power and evolution are concerned. Marxism rallies against it with its message of the paradise of the freedom rewon by socialism. At the same time it remains a product of middle-class spirit, because it considers the coming salvation as rationally demonstrable.

The key to secularization in Marxist eschatology is its dependence on society. The laborers' movement is bound to the conditions of its time, and its ideology remains determined by its contemporary social structure. Its belief and its eschatology are based upon the society of its time, that is, of bourgeoisie. This structure has to be destroyed, and Marxism is striving to reach that aim. Man is able to save himself — this was the bourgeois belief in the 19th and 20th centuries. Marxism adds only one variation to it: that the proletariat will fulfill the work of salvation, and in redeeming itself save the whole of mankind. Thus the proletariat is called to achieve true humanity for all people. Blood and tears will be the price, and millions will die. The proletariat has to suffer vicariously for the mankind of the future. (Lenin later on demanded that the right to lead the proletariat of the world belongs to the Russian nation because it had suffered so much.)

Marxist salvation will be reached by active brutality. Contrary to Christian eschatology the proletariat in its revolution must liquidate the wrong classes by violence. The fate of the fighting proletariat, as praised in poems, is described in a way which reminds one of a giant army of ants, ready to die in order to let a small remnant reach the wanted destination. Millions will sacrifice themselves, and there will be nothing but death and destruction; there will only be the hope that some of them, or at least their descendants, might gain the "laborers' paradise." This materialism holds no hope for the individual fighter; moreover, Marxist eschatology is like an immutable law of history, according to which most of the contemporary workers will be killed to attain the final aim. The individual can only be comforted with the knowledge that he is chosen by the historical moment for the great task of leading mankind to a higher step of evolution.

It is important that this moment in Marxism be recognized. This ideology does not, first of all, fight for better conditions of the individual or of oppressed classes but for the fulfillment of its basic idea. The materialistic understanding of love has no room for concern for people who are suffering now and want to be liberated from their miseries. It attacks everybody who wants to help the oppressed laborers at the moment by achieving better conditions of life for them. Marx's polemics against other socialist thinkers and organizations can be studied in the third chapter of the *Communist Manifesto*. The socialist rival is caricatured in as ugly terms as possible—thus, for example, Christianity is described as a servant of feudalism:

> As the parson has ever gone hand in hand with the landlord, so has clerical socialism with feudal socialism.
>
> Nothing is easier than to give Christian asceticism a socialist tinge. Has not Christianity declaimed against private property, against marriage, against the state? Has it not preached in the place of these charity and poverty, celibacy and mortification of the flesh, monastic life and Mother Church? Christian socialism is but the holy water with which the priest consecrates the vexation of the aristocrat. (P. 99)

We should not ignore the weaknesses and degeneration within Christianity. But the basic difference from Marxism cannot be overlooked: The understanding and practice of love is entirely different. The New Testament directs the believer to his neighbor: he is to be helped; he is to be cared for. There is no mechanical law which pushes mankind forward. The final aim cannot be reached with human power, energy, or brutality; it is God's gift. The Christian, therefore, is not subjected to a legal force like an oppressed slave but serves his Lord and thereby his environment freely in order to heal and to help overcome personal miseries.

To summarize the Christian conviction briefly we may say that:

(1) The present world will always be imperfect, for sin will remain; the basic change, therefore, will not come through human efforts but with God's new creation of heaven and earth after the present world has passed away. It would be an illusion and a forgetting of the Lord's clear words if we would hold to the hope that we are able to establish paradise already now on earth. On the other hand, Christian reality does not produce resignation or pessimism but offers a basis upon which positive and effective service for the world can be done.

(2) Christianity, namely, the Christian church as Christ's institution on earth, does not have as its primary aim the making of a better world—especially not by political revolution. The church's influence on state, society, etc. cannot be denied. It often is a real blessing to mankind. But it is the Lord's mandate that the church should proclaim the Gospel in order to reconcile man with his Creator and call him to trust in Christ Jesus the Savior. It can be proved in world history that the proclamation of the Biblical Gospel sets free those energies which best can help mankind in this time to overcome its manifold problems.

(3) Christian mission, the most important task of the church, will be done until God lets the Judgment Day arrive. This date,

determined and set by the Lord alone, will produce the final change for mankind.

POLITICAL METHODS

Theory and practice influence each other in Marxism. Its founder did not want to be a theoretical philosopher only but also a fighter for change in society. Clearly, this combination was especially effective in his political methods.

We have to keep in mind the political and mental situation of the working class in the middle of the 19th century. The existential conditions were bad. Disunion and competition among single groups within the proletariat hindered the establishment of an organized and powerful movement which could help overcome needs and miseries. Marx recognized that the coming class conflict had to be fought with political means. Therefore the proletariat had to be organized and trained. The Marxist theories had to be published, and the consciousness of the workers as a distinct and powerful class in themselves had to be cultivated. Thus organization and training created a labor movement with Marxist structure in the European countries. National differences did not prevent unity in thinking and action. The foundation of the Second International as a political instrument was a remarkable sign of the fact that Marxism had outgrown its task of scientific theorizing and had become a weapon in the class struggle of the proletariat. Whether Marxism could be refuted, therefore, was not important. Such a refutation was no longer able to destroy the power of that ideology over the worker. The workers believed in its truth in spite of the fact that only intellectual minorities were able to follow the complicated lines of Marxist thought.

In 1846 Marx voted for class alliances, especially for the alliance of the proletarian movement and the progressive bourgeoisie. According to the *Communist Manifesto* this alliance was of only temporary importance; after the victory over the proprietors, etc., was won, the proletariat would go on to abolish private property and thus liquidate the progressive bourgeoisie also. (Cf. p. 114 ff.)

Marx always considered the proletarian movement as an international movement. Capitalism existed independently of national borders and was, as an economic system, effective in every country. Therefore the destiny of the proletarian class was the same in every nation, and the socialization of private property had, consequently, to be the aim for the workers of all nations.

Was the class alliance a viable strategy for Marxism? The Communists tried to destroy Christianity and religion wherever they could seize the power of government. But the churches survived cruel persecutions. Millions of Christians were killed or punished with

47

banishment to forced labor camps. In Communism the highest number of Christian martyrs in world history was reached—a number which is still growing.

Christianity, however, remained a living movement. Its martyrdom shocked people in non-Communist countries who were interested in Marxism; and the same was the case with pagan world religions such as Islam. The Communist party discovered that existing Christians could be used as political instruments inside and outside their nations. The Soviets found out in World War II that the Russian Orthodox bishop Alexius supported the army and population of Leningrad when besieged by the Germans (he later received the high Communist medal of the red banner).

The Russian Orthodox membership in the World Council of Churches serves as an important political instrument for the Communists, whereby resolutions against inhumanities inside their countries can be prevented, while the brutalities in Western (capitalist) nations can be branded in public. There is a certain tolerance to be observed among the Communists with regard to Christianity in their areas; only a few exceptions need be named: Albania, Red China, and North Korea. Can this situation be explained through Marx's (and Lenin's) doctrine of class alliance?

It is difficult to find the correct answer. Persecution and oppression of Christianity has not stopped under the dictatorship of the proletariat but is now practised inside a certain framework. The final aim will not be reached by brutal acts, but the churches will die of starvation. Atheistic agitation and a strong limitation of Christian activities are to be the means. Often the church leaders themselves are Communists or sympathize with this ideology. Transgressions of applicable laws are punished. Christianity is not forbidden but is misused as a political instrument of Communist governments (a situation to which the churches in Europe and Russia have been accustomed for many centuries, since most of the monarchs in preceding periods also misused churches in their lands in order to rule the population more effectively).

The primary definition of class alliance is found in the theory of historical materialism: An alliance with the progressive bourgeoisie is possible in order to destroy the ruling capitalists. In principle, a class alliance cannot exist within the theory of dialectical materialism, for this ideology has a pseudo-religious character. Strict intolerance toward Christianity is its necessary consequence. The real situation, however, is quite different. The existence of an alliance, therefore, demonstrates that political pragmatism is necessary for Communism, too. This practical relation between the state and Christianity may best be defended by a variation in the theory of class alliance. Such a variation is only a compromise during a transition period and will not replace the ultimate and total elimination of Christianity and every religion. Otherwise Marxism would have destroyed one of the main pillars of its existence, namely, total atheistic materialism.

Chapter 3

Further Developments in Marxism

The last part of our treatise will paint a very rough sketch of different branches of Marxism which have emerged during the 20th century and Marxism's relationship to modern theological trends.

POLITICO-PHILOSOPHICAL BRANCHES

Marx's ideas and work created a new self-confidence among the working classes, which can be summarized with Willem Banning as follows:

a) The workmen are exploited by the capitalists because their work capacity creates capital growth.

b) The workers have to be organized in the class conflict (by labor unions and a political party); faithfulness to the movement is taken for granted by the conscientious worker.

c) The worker can be sure of his final victory; the development of private property toward a common proprietorship of the means of production is scientifically provable.

d) The class conflict has to be waged; therefore the bourgeois are always to be distrusted even if something agreeable is done or if there is cooperation in certain decisions.

e) Solidarity of the working class with all the necessary sacrifices is the supreme law in this class conflict; national solidarity is self-deception.

f) Trust in science with its knowledge, that is, trust in Darwin who proved the theory of evolution, and trust in Marx, who proved the future of the classless society and of socialist freedom for everybody.

g) Religion is passé; we need no belief in a beyond for our struggle, for a socialist society makes our lives rich. Our "god" is the liberation of mankind for which we are fighting.

However, it became evident at the end of the 19th century that neither society in the western European nations nor the socialist movement had developed according to Marx's theories. EDUARD BERNSTEIN (1850-1932), a convinced follower of Karl Marx, was led to conclude that Marxism had to be revised in several important areas. In his London exile Bernstein looked critically at his master's theory of the collapse of society and at historical materialism. The proletarian standard of living did not decrease but rather increased. Therefore the laborers' movement did not think first of a revolution, but of a social reform which could be accomplished through democratic and economic means. Bernstein wanted the revolutionary phrases to be eliminated: The Social Democratic Party (which stood for the Communists at that time) should, he thought, organize the working class politically in order to develop a democracy. The party should fight for reforms by which living conditions could be improved. Not pauperization but a growing social wealth would be in favor of the socialist movement. Bernstein attacked historical materialism because he thought that a rising class in a decaying society needed a healthy moral belief.

Bernstein's publications were sharply rejected by Marxist dogmaticians. They denied the necessity of changing Marx's ideological principles even when they were willing to accept Bernstein's ideas in practice. For Marx's theories of the coming disaster and revolution played the role of a confession of faith not only for the multitude of simple workers but also for the intellectuals.

A close friend of Bernstein was KARL KAUTSKY (1854-1938), who later on became his adversary. As the great theorist of orthodox German Marxism, he tried to connect Marx with Darwinian evolutionism. He was not aware of the differences between both materialist thinkers and did not have a developed understanding of dialectics. Kautsky believed in Marx's idea of the necessity of the revolution but wanted it to be without brutality or bloodshed. He thought that its final aims could be accomplished over a longer period of time. Intellectuals could also be involved in the socialist movement. After the proletariat had become the ruler, the state would no longer be a capitalist organization but would have changed into a socialist association.

The most important phenomenon in Marxism is the Russian development. Marx looked at western Europe and most especially at Germany in his search for a land in which the new society could be founded (cf. the *Communist Manifesto*, p. 116). He did so because those areas were highly industrialized. He was convinced that Russia was absolutely unable to accept his program. Eighty percent of its population lived in the country as farmers or farmhands, and almost the same number of people were illiterate. Serfdom had been abolished in 1861, and modern industry did not come into existence until after 1880. In the year 1900 the real Russian industrial proletariat amounted to about 3 million, while the whole Russian population of that time was about 160 million. How could a Marxist revolution be successful under those circumstances? Everything, even Christianity, was ordered by the government. It ruled through terror, and the population accepted that fact as something unavoidable in human life.

In 1883 a number of Russian socialists in exile founded the Russian Social Democratic Party in Geneva, Switzerland. Most of the members rejected the possibility of a successful revolution in Russia. Only two men were confident that it was possible: Lenin and Trotzki. At a congress in London in 1903 Lenin was able to win a majority of one vote for his program. Since that time the following two names have been used for the two groups composing Russian Communism: *Bolsheviki* (the majority), and Mensheviki (the minority). The brutal fights between the two groups signaled very early that the Russian branch of Marxism would have to be differentiated from western Marxism.

LENIN (Vladimir Ilych Ulyanov, 1870-1924) stood steadfastly upon the theories of Karl Marx as propounded in his *Communist Manifesto*. From this basis he attacked the German Marxists, including Karl Kautsky. The Russian situation forced him to develop an ideology in which it was possible to bypass the preconditions of historical materialism, the conditions created by industrial capitalism. The revolution could only be attained if he could win a group of revolutionaries who would be able to lead the multitudes according to his concept. It was he who introduced dialectical materialism in the form of an intolerant ideology. He interpreted the future "Dictatorship of the Proletariat" as a dictatorship of a minority over the majority, a dictatorship standing, not as in Marx's system at the end of industrial development, but at the beginning. The moral justification of the dictatorship was not based upon the will of the majority as Marx had based it. Rather, Lenin was forced to assert that his cadre as a minority was able to represent the interests of the multitude better than the multitude itself. Accordingly we must ask whether Lenin's system can really be considered a democracy, at least in theory; or is it rather an "enlightened despotism," in which terror is an essential element? Lenin might have been more radical than Marx as far as brutality was concerned, but the roots were to be found already in the principles of classic Marxist theory.

Lenin's theories received their final revision after he experienced the defeat of the revolution in 1905. The main points of that revision are as follows:

a) The party has to be a "formation of iron," the conscious elite of the revolutionaries, able in every respect to lead and to govern the multitude.

b) The theoretical confession of the party is the totalitarian ideology of dialectical materialism.

c) The party's practical task is the establishment and consolidation of the dictatorship of the proletariat.

d) It will lean on soviets, councils of workers, farmers, and soldiers during the revolution; these councils will be transformed to councils of farmers and laborers, thus forming a new political system after the conquest of power.

e) The revolution in Russia will be the fanfare for the worldwide revolution of the proletariat; this worldwide proletariat is beginning to fulfill the promises of the *Communist Manifesto*. The Russian proletariat is the advance guard of the worldwide proletariat.

Although Lenin gave more thought to the structures of the new socialist society after the changing revolution took place, the so-called "soviets" were not his invention. These councils of unorganized workers from the factories offered to arrange not only strikes but even the revolution in 1905. It is remarkable that these councils even came into being in a nation in which no organized, trained workers or proletariat could be found in those days.

Lenin developed Marx's and Engel's idea in which the new society has two phases: the socialist society, and the communist society. The first phase is reached when it is possible to conquer the state, establish the dictatorship of the proletariat and transform the ownership of the means of production from private property to common property. Once this has been achieved every member of the society fulfills a part of the social work and gets an equivalent amount of products in return. Differences of property may still exist, but it will be impossible for one individual to exploit another because there will be no private property as far as the means of production (the factories, the soil, etc.) are concerned. In spite of all the shortcomings which may still prevail in this transition society, two socialist principles will already have been realized: "Nobody will eat if he does not work," and "The same share of products for the same share of work." This society will still have a state, but it will be nothing more than a dying institution.

The second phase, the communist society, will be characterized by the fact that the state will have disappeared and the principle will be realized "from everybody according to his abilities, to everybody according to his needs." Lenin warned strongly of the necessity of extending the first period. Labor and consumption would have to be controlled by the community and the state. The control would begin with the removal of the capitalists, and it would be performed not by a state of officers but by a state of armed workers.

After a period of brutal struggle STALIN (Iosif Vissarionovich or Dzhugashvili, 1879-1953) was given the mandate to be Lenin's successor. Lenin's hope that the Russian revolution would be the signal for the revolution of the world proletariat had not been realized. Stalin, therefore, concentrated his energy on the Russian revolution: industrialization, electrification, collectivization, centralization. A system of terror was established which not only served as an instrument of controlling hostile classes but also for disposing of Stalin's personal enemies and rivals in the Communist party.

According to Stalin, three classes exist during the transition period: the workers, the citizens, and the farmers. The working class conquered the state and became the ruling class. The small farmers belong to the working class and must therefore be transformed into "colchose-farmers," while the larger farmers, the capitalists, must be liquidated as was the middle class. The confrontation of the workers and the small farmers with the larger farmers, industrialists, and businessmen, is the moving power for class conflict in the transition society.

Stalin can also be considered the founder of strongly nationalistic Russian Communism. He ordered the whole Russian history to be re-written. Certain national heroes had to be considered his predecessors, including Czar Peter the First. Panslavism can also be attributed to Stalin's nationalistic Communism. Moscow invited and arranged several Panslavic conferences during the war. These conferences praised the Russian nation as the foremost leader in the fight for freedom. The Russian Orthodox Church remains convinced that Christ, when He comes again, will arrive as a Slav. Moscow will then serve as the spiritual leader of all nations and as the third Metropol after Rome and Byzantium. Stalin pragmatically gave support to these ideas, although he did not personally believe them.

The last major group of Marxist thinkers to be considered here is the French. The writings of the younger Marx serve as the basis for a number of intellectual individuals who for several reasons have left the Communist party but still consider themselves to be true Marxists. —HENRI LEFEBVRE is critical of the sophisticated explanations of materialism as "movement of matter (DIAMAT)." Stalin introduced a dogmatism which is opposed to Marx's basic thought; and the Russian state must be seen as being in reality in opposition to Marx's under-standing of the future society. —PIERRE FOUGEYROLLAS who left the Communist party after the Hungarian riots of 1956, wants to reform Marxism to fit our present social problems. Thereby it will be possible to make this ideology a liberating and inspiring power once more. A weakness of Marxism today is its frequent use as a sociological theory or as a scientific method. "Ideology" for Fougeyrollas does not mean a system closed in itself but a teaching of value *(Wertlehre)*. The times of absolute and all-encompassing dogmas are gone. He adopts Marx's terms "social righteousness" and "freedom," and demands that they be realized in modern society. This is to be accomplished by a technocratic and collectivistic concept within the managements of factories, of government and its apparatus, and even in the area of hought. — Lefebvre and Fougeyrollas are avowed atheists. Yet their indebtedness to Marx as a spiritual father (especially in the case of Fougeyrollas or Proudhon) is open to question.

The most important group within the French Communists seeks to combine Marxism and existentialism. — JEAN PAUL SARTRE, a well-known philosopher and acknowledged atheist, views the class conflict against the bourgeoisie as ethically vindicated. He therefore offers many motives for a radical revolutionary concept while at the same time interceding for sovereign human freedom as an effective power in the world. Russian Communism negated existential freedom, is stamped by dogmatism, and is as absolute as real ontology. Sartre does not support it. He thinks that Marxism is the truth of our time, especially for poor nations or peoples, but its insufficient anthropology needs to be complemented and corrected. Materialism must be replaced by man as the real starting point, and this can only be accomplished by the sovereign freedom of the individual. Sartre's thoughts presuppose that Marxism will give up its claim of being a totalitarian ideology.

SIMONE DE BEAUVOIR wrote that the proletariat still has to decide whether it will be active and revolutionary, or whether it will be passive and thus entrapped by the capitalists in a dormant state. It is not possible to distinguish between the "true" and the "false" proletariat. We possess only the ideal for the proletariat, not the actual reality, unless we maintain this distinction.

MERLEAU-PONTI tries to demonstrate that the young Marx was an existentialist: he tried to conquer freedom by using every means in his power, although he knew the risk connected with such an attempt. Environment and neighbor are the necessary preconditions for a being to become man. He can only find justification for his own existence in the existence of others. Moral interest inside each man raises the urgent question of the destiny of others. Every man flees from himself if he tries to escape this question. — All these theories can hardly be combined with the Marxism of Soviet ideology. Indeed, *that* Marxism can only be interpreted by the party, the highest authority.

After having considered some developments of Marxism in the 20th century, it may be asked if any of them can be considered a legitimate child of that ideology. Some of them are quite the opposite of others (for example, Lenin against Bernstein and Kautsky; or Lefebvre and Sartre as opposed to DIAMAT). It is obvious that especially the French socialists use Marxist ideas only insofar as they fit their own existential understanding of man, the world, and society. Bernstein was impressed by the fact that Marx's prophetic statements were not fulfilled; while Lenin was forced to transform Marxism to fit the conditions of Russian society. This shows that Marx's system gave strong impulse to differing movements and philosophies even as it brought forth daughter ideologies and movements. It was not always adopted as a whole. It could not be completely adopted, for it was bound to its own times. Based upon a materialistic anthropology, it is subject to the change of human understanding dependent on the respective "Zeitgeist." We may even ask if Marx developed a system closed in itself. The differentiation between the younger and older Marx thought so necessary by some scholars of Marxism gives validity to such a question.

It would seem obvious that there is no possible way to combine Marxism and Christianity. However, since there are some facts which appear to contradict this assertion, we will have to examine them more closely in the final discussion.

MARXISM AND MODERN THEOLOGICAL TRENDS

It is not possible at the moment to give more than a brief overview of this question. This is simply because with this topic we enter an area which is yet to be fully explored.

(Some material will be appearing shortly, that is, an announced book will give the research results of an investigation of the relationship of Karl Barth to Marxism, by Friedrich Wilhelm Marquardt. Also Klaus Bockmühl's second and third parts of his publication *Atheismus in der Christenheit — Anfechtung und Ueberwindung,* is now being printed.)

There are dialogues between Christian theologians and Marxists on both sides of the Iron Curtain. The Prague Conference is perhaps the best known institution. While assuming that both sides hope for positive results we must ask if the members are thinking in terms of agreement between Christianity and Marxism or of attempted conversion by one side of the other. Heavy crises inside the Prague Peace Conference demonstrate that this institution wants to use Christian theologians for Communist aims. In fact, most of the theologians now involved in this organization are persons who are frankly sympathetic toward Marxism and Eastern Communism.

Friedrich Wilhelm Marquardt wrote that Karl Barth used the term "revolution" (for example, *Revolution Gottes*) seriously in his commentary on Romans. "The exegesis of Romans 13 in his first edition is, as we previously discovered, a highly spirited disputation on Lenin's contribution on state and revolution, the essential aspects of which were transferred by Barth from the revolutionary subject of the proletariat to the subversive subject of the Christian congregation." Barth therefore defines "state" (even *Rechtsstaat*) as bad in itself. It is brutal power (cf. also Barth's definition of "potentia" as absolute ethically indifferent power). Barth thought of the mortifying state on Marxist-Leninist lines, although he did not agree with Lenin that the dictatorship of the proletariat would be more righteous than the rule of its predecessors. — Marquardt does not want to show that Barth's whole heology has to be interpreted in comparison with basic Marxist houghts; but he does assert that real Marxist aspects were of influence n Barth's theological system.

Klaus Bockmühl offers us a similar picture in his analysis of Barth's dogmatic principles. Together with the Marxist philosopher Milan Machovec, Bockmühl states that Barth's de-objectification of theological terms and statements pushes God into a sphere which can never be reached by any struggle inside this world. Dialectical theology asserts that there is no way from man to God because men are atheists and will, with the ongoing process of the socialist revolution, increasingly reject any God. Dialectical theology thereby proves, according to Machovec, that the Marxist criticism of religion is correct when it states that every theology is a mystic expression of the social evolution of a crisis. "The 'real core' of the thesis that there is an infinite qualitative difference between God and world, this radical dualism, has to be understood as the mystified definition of the truth of atheism."

Machovec considers it progress when Barth liberated the secular world from God for man. For this Marxist thinker Barth is an intermediate step on the way from Christian belief to atheistic humanism. And Klaus Bockmühl concludes that the de-objectification of dialectical theology destroys every possibility of defending the basic Biblical dogmas against Marxist Communism: "A theology of God's unreality with regard to the world as offered by Barth or Bultmann perverts the essential moment of Christian revelation and is able to annihilate theology and the church by degrees."

But Bockmühl admits that the basic intention of Barth's theological concept is often defused—especially in the older Barth—by the fact that this theologian did not stop studying the Holy Scriptures and sought constantly for a combination with Biblical truth. He entered the Swiss Socialist Party in 1915. That is to say that he was already practising a political loyalty before he began to develop his theological system. He was influenced by religious socialists such as Ragaz and Kutter. All these factors may help to make Barth's position understandable, especially in our own age when some ideas in his writings function as an open door for Marxism.

There is no doubt that RUDOLF BULTMANN's theological system serves as a transition to atheism for many young theologians. His existentialist program of demythologizing the New Testament leads to a de-objectification of the Christian message by other means. Bultmann is not a Marxist, and like Barth he surely does not want to be regarded as an atheist. However we cannot ignore the fact that the consequences of his system leave nothing of Christianity except a certain religious feeling inside man brought forth by the "existential interpretation" of the Biblical texts. How far Bultmann's disciples developed this anthropocentric method is common knowledge. His and Gogarten's concepts would consequently lead to a "God is dead" theology which did nothing to hinder Marxism from entering the whole field. Joachim Kahl's publication, *Das Elend des Christentums*, demonstrates the lack of continuity in the basis of that theology brought to light by the Marxist critique of religion.

Oscar Cullman is correct when he castigates the intention of Bultmann and his school to say that there is nothing historical in the basic Christian message and that it is not necessary to proclaim the Lord's saving deeds as historical facts. This makes Christianity a religion like many others and it is a triumph for Marxism when it is confirmed by theologians who themselves judge Christianity like every other religious phenomenon.

What is said by those theologians is not Christian at all. It is rather an attempt to hold ground for the importance and right to existence of a certain theology which has emptied itself of its Christian contents by replacing them with an anthropocentric religiosity. It is typical that as a consequence of such a change the right comprehension of the Gospel is always lost, and a legal understanding of man's belief and activity dominates. Man's connection with God is less important than his activity for his neighbor and his world, for the Law is especially effective in this area. But when it develops upon the basis of legal demand, love *(agape)* is no longer an evangelical charisma.

The THEOLOGY OF REVOLUTION is the most recent arrival in the Christian camp. Conversion is seen as one of the keystones. Is it really only the return of individuals, or does conversion at the same time mean a visible change in social conditions? Karl Barth in his *Kirchliche Dogmatik* (IV/2, p. 626 ff.) tried to demonstrate that conversion is always effective with regard to man's spiritual and social existence. He wanted to ward off the understanding of conversion as only an individual act and accordingly emphasized the social consequences as most important. Some followers of the theology of revolution refer to Barth.

Joachim Staedtke admits that only some younger theologians from the left wing had pleaded for a conversion of structures. Most of the representatives of the group deny the possibility that Christian theology can speak in that way. But he does mention Harvey Cox's agreement with Marx's conviction that man's conversion is dependent on certain created objective preconditions. Abolition of private property is necessary for Marx if man's wrong consciousness is to be corrected. Cox says that subversion, revolution, *"katastrophe,"* is the essential precondition of penance and conversion. This subversion is brought by God's kingdom *or*(!) by the secular city. In other words a new social situation has to appear if the call to repentance is to be effective.

Consequently one can show the connection to a theology such as that represented chiefly by Hoekendijk, Hollenweger, and others, in which Christian mission activity has to be found first of all at places of social, political, and economic conflict ("situationalism"). A close similarity with basic Marxist ideas is evident. And an interest in an accord with Communism can be observed at those points.

It will be very difficult to prove any great contrast between Marxism and this theology of revolution. It is true that conversion cannot be understood as a selfish individual event which necessarily has no positive consequences for our social and even for our political environment. But at the same time the Biblical truth has to be emphasized that sanctification follows justification. Everything follows justification. Everything belongs to sanctification which stands under the effectiveness of Christian love.

The approaches which modern theological systems make to Marxism do not really satisfy Communism. The respective theologians are acknowledged and even honored according to the rule of "class alliance," but no more than that. The Czech Marxist philosopher Machovec views the Prague Peace Conference as an instrument of Soviet ideological strategy. Adalbert Hudak quotes a contribution from the Moscow periodical *Voprosy Filosofii* (11/1968, p. 95-103): "Although modern theology has tried to combine the contradictions between religion and science it has not been able to eliminate the contradictions between belief and rational thinking."

Marxism considers the definition of God in modern theology as a form of behavior in humanity and as a further step to theology's own liquidation. The end will come just as it did in alchemy. Just as there was no stone of the wise men so there is no God. When modern theology seeks to preserve religion and the church by unlimited accommodation, it undermines the basis of all religions and creates an unbridgeable gap between itself and faithful believers. "The way of total subjectivation of belief is at the same time the way toward its annihilation." Modern theology demonstrates the disintegration and decomposition of religion "at the same moment that it proves its incapacity for offering an adequate solution of present spiritual and social problems."

However, the theological results presented by Manfred Mezger, John A. T. Robinson, Herbert Braun, and others have to be acknowledged by Marxism. These results, namely the abolition of a real belief in God and the growth of positive attitudes toward materialistic socialism, grant new perspectives for the cooperation of nominal Christians and Marxists with respect to solving basic questions of our time, especially questions related to the fight against Western imperialism, militarism, war, and political clericalism. It therefore is the task of the Marxists to support the ongoing process inside modern theology which moves from Christian presuppositions toward humanistic and progressive consequences. Marxism has the double duty of rejecting any unprovable theoretical claims (for example, the assertion that God is a certain kind of humanity) and of cooperating with modernist theologians (because they emphasize man's responsibility in his social existence through their progressive actions).

Ralph L. Moellering states in his contribution, "The Christian-Marxist Dialog: Spurious or Authentic?" that such a dialog can under certain circumstances make sense:

> If Marxism is open to repudiate particular historical manifestations of communism like Stalinism or Maoism and revises and reinterprets earlier theories, while Christians find their assurance of salvation in justification by faith as a matter of divine grace and are not attached to a specific or static *Weltanschauung*, if minds are not closed to innovation and change, then perhaps dialog can be helpful and fruitful (*Concordia Theological Monthly*, Jan. 1971, p. 44).

There are many preconditions here which make the statement quite theoretical. There is hope, however, if we remember the many sects and diverging groups inside the Marxist family. Not every group within Marxism is (fully) based upon dialectical materialism. Witness philosophers such as Ernst Bloch or Jean Paul Sartre. Banning once demonstrated the problem of a divided Marxism: When someone begins his speech with the words, "I, as a Marxist . . .", he is then to be asked, "What kind of Marxism do you represent?"

Not everyone who considers himself such can be judged a real Marxist. The decision must be made on his attitude toward the principles of Marx's anthropology. Whenever he gives a positive yes to exclusive materialistic naturalism it is clear that any dialog with such a Marxist will be a dialog with a pseudo-religion and nothing else.

It is necessary, of course, to understand Christian belief properly, too. The Gospel of Jesus Christ, redemption and justification, is the very core of Christianity, but it is not the whole of Christianity. The content of the First Article of the Apostles' Creed also belongs to the Christian faith. This prevents Christians from attempting to make decisions in political, social, or economic areas apart from their faith in and responsibility to Christ their Lord.

Marxism is first of all a rejection of God's rule over the world; this stamps it as atheism. Klaus Bockmühl states: "Atheism often cannot be considered to be simply an intellectual cosmological decision based upon observation and insight, but much rather an existential-historical decision made before any observation of reality took place."

This is true. We therefore dare not nourish any illusions when we consider our relationship to Marxism.

LITERATURE

Banning, Willem. *Karl Marx. Leben, Lehre und Bedeutung.* München, 1966.

Barth, Karl. *Der Roemerbrief.* 4. Auflage, München, 1924.

_____. *Christengemeinde und Buergergemeinde.* München, 1946.

_____. *Dogmatik im Grundriss.* 2. Auflage, München, 1949.

_____. *Kirchliche Dogmatik.* Band IV/2. Zürich, 1955.

Bloch, Ernst. *Religion im Erbe.* München, 1967.

Bockmühl, Klaus. *Leiblichkeit und Gesellschaft.* Studien zur Religionskritik und Anthropologie im Frühwerk von Ludwig Feuerbach und Karl Marx. Göttingen, 1961.

_____. *Atheismus in der Christenheit. Anfechtung und Ueberwindung.* 1. Teil: Die Unwirklichkeit Gottes in Theologie und Kirche. Wuppertal, 1969.

Bultmann, Rudolf. "Neues Testament und Mythologie. Das Problem der Entmythologisierung der neutestamentlichen Verkündigung." In *Kerygma und Mythos I,* S. 15 ff. Hamburg, 1948.

Cox, Harvey G. *Stadt ohne Gott?* 3. Auflage. Stuttgart, 1967.

Cullmann, Oscar. *Heil als Geschichte.* 2. Auflage. Tübingen, 1967.

Fetscher, Iring. "Die Hoffnung der Sowjetmarxisten auf den Kommunismus." In *Die Hoffnungen unserer Zeit,* S. 75 ff. München, 1964.

_____. *Marx-Engels III und IV.* Studienausgabe. Frankfurt, 1966.

_____. "Marxismus." In *Evangelisches Staatslexikon,* Col. 1277 ff. Stuttgart, 1966.

Girock, Hans-Joachim, ed. *Partner von morgen? Das Gespraech zwischen Christentum und marxistischem Atheismus.* Stuttgart, 1968.

Gollwitzer, Helmut. " . . . *Und fuehren, wohin du nicht willst." Bericht einer Gefangenschaft.* München, 1951.

_____. *Die marxistische Religionskritik und der christliche Glaube.* 3. Auflage, München, 1970.

_____. *Krummes Holz — aufrechter Gang. Zur Frage nach dem Sinn des Lebens.* 2. Auflage, München, 1971.

Hudak, Adalbert. "Die moderne Theologie im Lichte der marxistischen Philosophie." In *Nachrichten der Notgemeinschaft Evangelischer Deutscher,* Bernhausen, April 1971, S. 4 ff.

Jüchen, Aurel von. *Atheismus in West und Ost.* Berlin, 1968.

Kahl, Joachim. *Das Elend des Christentums, oder: Plaedoyer fuer eine Humanitaet ohne Gott.* Reinbek, 1968.

Lenin, V. I. *Ausgewaehlte Werke in zwei Baenden.* Moskau, 1946.

Lindberg, Carter. "Luther and Feuerbach." In *Sixteenth Century Essays and Studies,* vol. l. 107 ff. St. Louis, Mo., 1970.

Marquardt, Friedrich Wilhelm. "Der Götze wackelt — Der Generalangriff aus dem Römerbrief." In *Portraet eines Theologen — Stimmt unser Bild von Karl Barth?* S. 11 ff. Stuttgart, 1970.

_____. "Notwendige Scheidungen und Entscheidungen in der Theologie Karl Barths." In *Portraet eines Theologen . . .* S. 29 ff.

_____. "Exegese und Dogmatik in Karl Barths Theologie." In Karl Barth, *Die Kirchliche Dogmatik.* Registerband, S. 649 ff. Zürich, 1970.

Marx, Karl. *Die Fruehschriften,* herausgegeben von Siegfried Landshut. Stuttgart, 1968. (Abbrev.: Kroener.)

Marx, Karl / Engels, Friedrich. *Manifest der Kommunistischen Partei.* Berlin, 1948. *The Communist Manifesto.* New York, 1964. (Used for citations.)

Moellering, Ralph L. "The Christian-Marxist Dialog: Spurious or Authentic? In *Concordia Theological Monthly.* St. Louis, Mo., Jan. 1971, p. 25 ff.

Moltmann, Jürgen. *Umkehr zur Zukunft.* München, 1970.

Ratschow, Karl Heinz. *Atheismus im Christentum? Eine Auseinandersetzung mit Ernst Bloch.* 2. Auflage. Gütersloh, 1971.

Staedtke, Joachim. "Busze und Bekehrung in der Theologie der Revolution." In *Christsein in einer pluralistischen Gesellschaft,* S. 218 ff. Hamburg, 1971.

Stalin, J. *Fragen des Leninismus.* Moskau, 1947.

Thier, Erich. *Die Kirche und die soziale Frage.* Gütersloh, 1950.

_____. *Das Menschenbild des jungen Marx.* Göttingen, 1957.

Troeltsch, Ernst. *Die Sozialphilosophie des Christentums.* Gotha, 1922.

Weber, Max. *Die protestantische Ethik I und II,* herausgegeben von Johannes Winckelmann. München, 1965/1968.

Religion

CONTEMPORARY THEOLOGY SERIES

The theological issues and movements of our time are every-thing but dull and dry. Pulsating, controversial, vibrant, politically and culturally influential—they require of the concerned theologian serious study and scrutiny.

The Contemporary Theology Series now provides a reliable means to examine today's theological scene. Each monograph supplies theological information, analysis, commentary, and perspective from the author's field of interest. The scholarly substance of a current theological issue so you can validly analyze and evaluate it.

SERIES I

THE APOSTOLIC SCRIPTURES, David Scaer
THE ETHICS OF REVOLUTION, Martin Scharlemann
IT IS WRITTEN, Jacob A. O. Preus
THE LUTHERAN WORLD FEDERATION TODAY,
  David Scaer
THE MINISTRY AND THE MINISTRY OF WOMEN,
  Peter Brunner

SERIES II

A CHRISTIAN VIEW OF ABORTION, John W. Klotz
FORM CRITICISM REEXAMINED, Walter A. Maier
THE LORD'S SUPPER TODAY, Werner Elert
MARXISM AND CHRISTIANITY, Hans-Lutz Poetsch
UNITY AND FELLOWSHIP AND ECUMENICITY,
  Henry Hamann

CONCORDIA
PUBLISHING | HOUSE
3558 SOUTH JEFFERSON AVENUE
SAINT LOUIS, MISSOURI 63118

Printed in U. S. A.

12-2563
ISBN 0-570-06724-3

DATE DUE

APR 8 1991			
MAR 0 3 1994			
12/03/02			